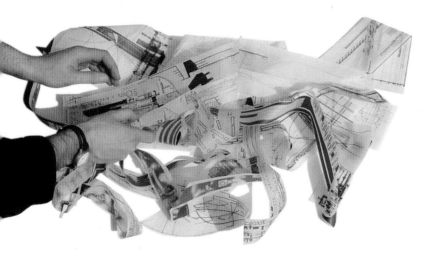

metis

urban

cartographies

Mark Dorrian and Adrian Hawker

introduction
Postscript
as
Pretext

the fox and the octopus

We first used the term metis as tutors, in conjunction with a final-year design project at the University of Edinburgh.[1] In this context, students were invited to make, using actual materials, a full-scale construction of a part of a project upon which they had worked for the previous seven months. Beyond being a construction study, this called for responses that would reflect and exploit the potentialities and powers of the 'object', whether considered iconic, erotic, or otherwise. In this context, metis seemed to offer a way of circumventing modes of talking about making in terms of an ethics of craftsmanship or truth to materials. In place of honesty, metis introduced notions of guile, cunning, and trickery; but also of seeing and seizing the particular possibilities imminent in a certain milieu or context. Metis did not operate through principles formulated in advance and applied to stable situations, but rather involved a kind of opportunism glimpsed in a fluctuating world. Certainly it invoked a high degree of craftsmanship (the artificer Daedalus being the emblematic metis-man), but this was a craftsmanship that tended to efface rather than display itself, whether in the necessarily illusionistic structure of the hunting trap or the magical auratic object.

In their study of metis in Greek culture, Jean-Pierre Vernant and Marcel Detienne spelled out its operation in terms, that seemed to us, to have a real contemporary relevance. "Its field of application", they wrote, "is the world of movement, of multiplicity and of ambiguity. It bears on fluid situations which are constantly changing and which at every moment combine contrary features and forces that are opposed to each other."[2] Always immersed in practical operations and without the assumption of the privileged overview (as its journey is only known at the end, its pretexts are only ever postscripts), it progresses by hunch and anticipation, by "feeling its way and guessing".[3] If an approach grounded in assumptions of certitude imperiously establishes frameworks or drives ways through, metis, as a situational practice, can only use what is at hand to establish shifting orientations in a mobile environment which it must attempt to channel: it dissimulates, doubles back, circumambulates, tacks, and will try, if it can, to trap the wind in a bag.

In Greek thought, the fox and the octopus were the creatures which best demonstrated and symbolised metis. The fox because of its ability to reverse itself, to suddenly alternate between opposing conditions. Playing dead, it tempts other creatures to approach before springing to life. The octopus because of its polymorphy, which is also a polysemy. It is a "living knot" or labyrinth which can blend into its background and whose indeterminacy is epitomised in the black stain of ink which it secretes.[4]

cartography and cacography

One of the major interests of the work presented in this book is the performative possibilities inherent in the 'representational archive' – the maps, site drawings, photographs, historical documents, etc. – through which any architectural project, even prior to its design, presents itself. Crucially, it insists upon representation as the true 'site' of the architectural project. Architects tend to talk as if they worked directly upon architecture's physical sites. But this is almost never the case. Instead they work upon representations through which those sites are mediated and which come to describe and direct actions to be taken upon them. Even if its implications have rarely been pursued, historically this has served to underwrite definitions of architecture: architecture is something that is communicated; it is worked out in advance, follows a design (and therefore deals in representation) and this distinguishes it from, so the story (unproblematically) tends to go, the brute immediacy of mere building, the vernacular, etc..

The representational codes within which projects are constituted and pursued are not neutral but value-laden: they bring selected elements in certain ways into the "architect's field of visibility" while hiding others.[5] The Ordnance Survey map, for example, emerged historically within the horizon of military, legal, and economic concerns, and these underpin its representational form. Once the vision it presents has been denaturalised – once, that is, we no longer understand it as a neutral device which conveys the site 'in itself' – the question arises as to how one might work with it to extract other stories, to brush it against its grain. Two possibilities come to mind. One might return to the territory in order to remap and hence remake it according to a different set of values and procedures which are then used to infiltrate, unsettle and collapse the source map.[6] This is the fox's strategy (of reversal). Equally, one might become interested in the pathologies of the map, in those moments where the representation seems to lose itself, and in the architectural possibilities they contain. One could, in other words, treat it as a performative document on the basis of a cacography.[7] To do this, according to Michel Serres, we would need to turn our attention to stammerings, mispronunciations, dysphonics, background noise, jamming, statics, cut-offs, hyteresis and interruptions in the communication. Everything, that is, where representation thought as identity fails in the face of its material, empirical instantiation: where the line has broken because of a printing failure, or the ink has bled... Here we are in the realm of the octopus. Legibility has lapsed; codes of representation and reading have become unhinged; chance, polysemy and a new interpretive demand have entered.

repetition... hesitation... deviation

These projects attempt, in working upon their constitutive representational archives, to exploit the iterability of architectural representation and, in particular, the "logic which links repetition to alterity".[8] More specifically, the emphasis falls upon the repetition as a reperformance which produces sequences of differential effects; from these opportunities unfold. This defamiliarisation is akin to the uncanny effect of the word which, by being whispered over and over again, is gradually detached from its meaning until only its strange materiality is experienced like clay in one's mouth.

This alterity in repetition occurs in two ways. On one hand, through a recontextualising whereby the representation becomes grafted into a new condition. The project for Ottawa is patterned by this approach. Maps representing different chronologies are grafted into one another; the property lines which striate the site are set into the aerial photograph; the aerial photograph, remade on the basis of these lines, is grafted onto the map; and the resultant assemblage is resituated, and reperformed, within the context of the narratives which are the prompt for a graphic recoding of the city. This is perhaps most clearly seen in the strip which travels through and reperforms the existing Canadian parliament building before being gathered by the fold mechanisms, as a 'double', and sedimented within the project's site: the fox, again. And on the other hand, by the effects that come from the processes and technologies of copying; the moments in which the 'noise' of transmission is felt and the image breaks down; events which would, in the last instance, make each repetition specific and guarantee it a radical unrepeatability. In opposition to any tendency to see images as having a pristine virtuality, the stress here is upon the specific material instantiation; and this is defined as much by the material 'support' of the image (paper, canvas, electronic screen, etc.) as it is by the mode of transmission and 'materiality' of the image itself. These materialities, which are the conditions of possibility of the image, simultaneously unfold patterns of (productive) interference. In the Ottawa project this is, to take two examples, played out through the very material manipulation of the paper strips (the material support of the image makes certain procedures available while disqualifying others) and in the attention paid to the dissolution of the aerial photographic image. More generally, interference in the image becomes akin to the "rhinoceros skin seen through microscope" which Deleuze discusses with reference to Francis Bacon: cacography (the ink cloud of the octopus) is like the "catastrophe" upon the painting's surface which deterritorialises it and returns it to a productive moment that, while thickly modulated, is prior to meaning.[9]

Of all the projects presented here, the theme of repetition is most insistent in the 'mimetic urbanism' proposal for Verona. Using a suggestion given in the brief that the area of Verona South be considered a double of the old city, the project developed using a sequence of transformational copying strategies. The animation frames are thought of

10

as describing, in a quasi-mathematical sense, an iterative process. We start at a point –
at the source element, which is like a 'guess' in its relationship to its final configuration –
and move via transformational iterative stages toward a destination. The iteration spans
between two values: the 'guess' and the 'solution'.

To describe the opportunities within representation and its failure that these projects try
to seize does not account for the particular decisions taken. How were the choices made?
How were trajectories established within the field of possibilities offered? This can only be
a question of judgement and anticipation in which the full range of architecture's concerns
must participate. The good decision is the most connective: the one which extends,
proliferates, ramifies, and most compellingly implicates architecture. Many preoccupations
and enthusiasms underlie this work, but perhaps the most important have been the urges
to locate the projects within an urban imaginary and to modulate architectural space in
its interconnectedness from the urban assemblage to the detail.

once more with feeling

Odysseus, a remarkable metis-man (who was even described as an "octopus") was an
equally remarkable traveller. The image of the traveller runs through these projects, from
Latitude and Longitude Resolved to the Cabinet of the City in which the Grand Tourist
reappears. The traveller, as well as being a cipher for the uncertain, incremental,
negotiated processes from which these projects emerge, is the paradigmatic performer,
manipulator, and misuser of maps whose pristine qualities soon give way to wears and
tears and strange diversions as they are misfolded, ripped and torn, hung out as a shelter
and up to dry. And of course the traveller is also a collector (as was – to take us back to
the beginning – John Soane), an accumulator of souvenirs (another representational
archive) through which the journey may be re-membered but from which other itineraries
are sure to be dreamt and drawn.[10]

1   We were introduced to it by Alberto Pérez-Gómez's essay "The Myth of Daedalus" in *AA Files*, 10, 1985, pp. 49-52.

2   Vernant, Jean-Pierre and Marcel Detienne, *Cunning Intelligence in Greek Culture and Society*, Janet Lloyd, trans., Chicago and London: University of Chicago Press, 1991, p. 20.

3   Vernant, *Cunning*, p. 4.

4   Vernant, *Cunning*, pp. 34-39.

5   "Architectural drawing affects what might be called the architect's field of visibility. It makes it possible to see some things more clearly by suppressing other things... We have to understand architectural drawing as something that defines the things it transmits. It is not a neutral vehicle transporting conceptions into objects, but a medium that carries and distributes information in a particular mode." Evans, Robin, "The Developed Surface: An Enquiry into the Brief Life of an Eighteenth-Century Drawing Technique", *Translations from Drawing to Building and Other Essays*, London: Architectural Association, 1997, pp. 194-231, (199).

6   Dorrian, Mark, "Mapping as an Architectural Strategy", forthcoming in Pousin, Frédéric, ed., *Figurations/Transferts: Les figures de la ville dans le développement des savoirs et l'intervention spatiale*, Paris: CNRS, 2003. Also, Corner, James, "The Agency of Mapping: Speculation, Critique and Invention" in Cosgrove, D, ed., *Mappings*, London: Reaktion Books, 1999, pp. 213-252.

7   Serres, Michel, "Platonic Dialogue" in *Hermes: Literature, Science, Philosophy*, Harari, Josué V and David F Bell, trans., Baltimore and London: John Hopkins University Press, 1982, pp. 65-70, (66).

8   Derrida, Jacques, "Signature Event Context" in *Margins of Philosophy*, Alan Bass, trans., Brighton: Harvester Press, 1982, pp. 307-330 (315).

9   While not "manual" in the sense that Deleuze discusses, these interruptions in the image also "reveal the intrusion of another world into the visual world of figuration. To some extent they remove the [image] from the optical organisation that already governed it and made it figurative in advance... we can no longer see anything, as in a catastrophe or chaos." Deleuze, Gilles, "The Diagram" in *The Deleuze Reader*, Constatin V Boundas, ed., New York: Columbia University Press, 1993, pp. 193-200 (194).

10 Soane, in whose country house Latitude and Longitude Resolved was installed, was both a fox and an octopus. On his museum as a topography of travel see Tafuri, Manfredo, "'The Wicked Architect': G B Piranesi, Heterotopia, and the Voyage" in *The Sphere and the Labyrinth: Avant-Gardes and Architecture from Piranesi to the 1970s*, Pellegrino d'Acierno and Robert Connolly, trans., Cambridge, MA and London: MIT Press, 1987 pp. 25-54 (40).

metis

urba

carto

Latit

Latitude and Longitude Resolved

Britannia Basin – Manchester
Mimetic Urbanism – Verona
Micro Urbanism – Ottawa
Cabinet of the City – Rome

Based upon the theme of the Grand Tour, this installation
was designed for the gallery of the Institut Français
d'Ecosse in Edinburgh which occupies a town house in an
area of the city known as the Moray Estate. Developed
after 1822 to designs by James Gillespie Graham, this lies
close to the city centre, to the north-west of James Craig's
first New Town.

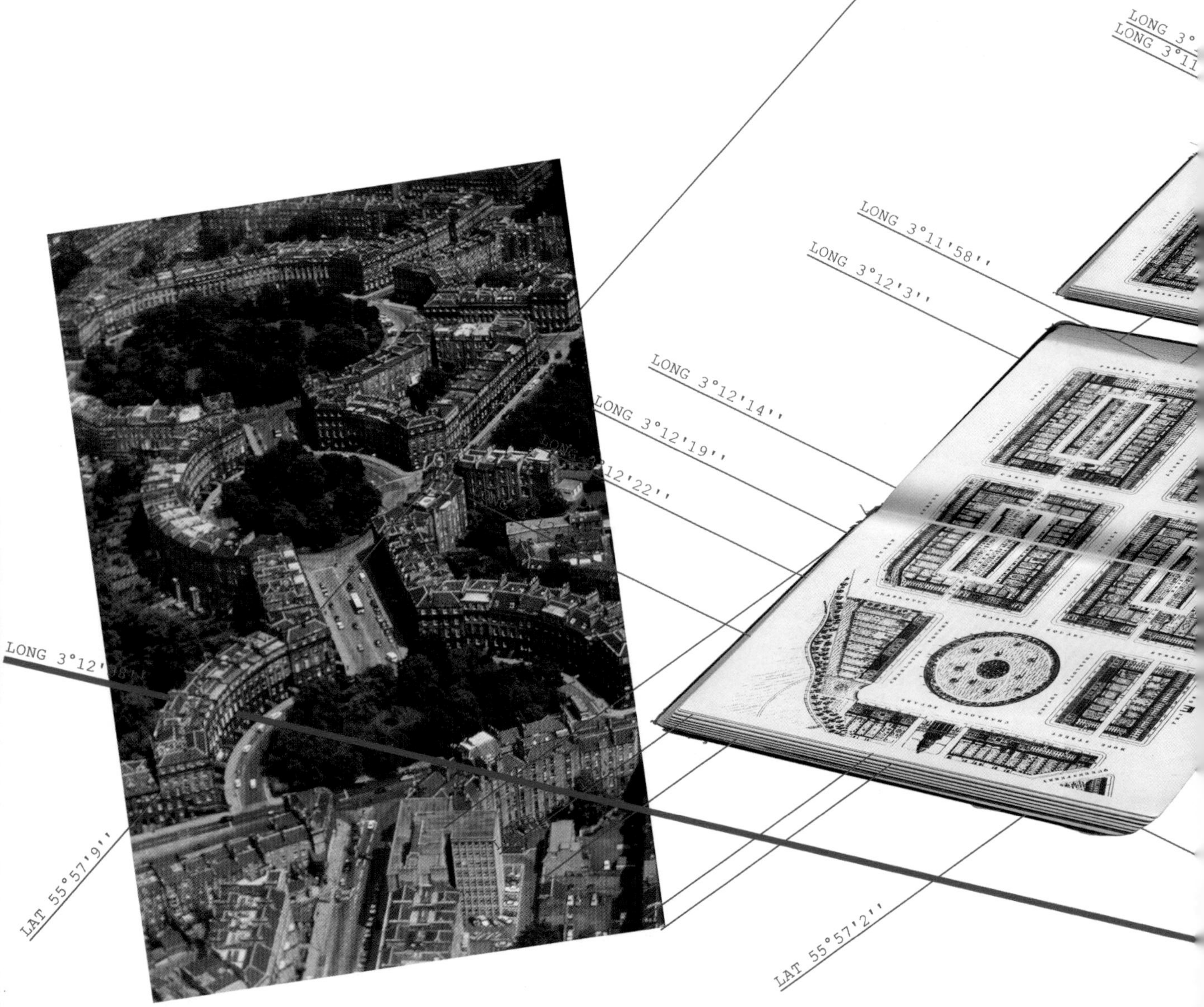

LONG 3°
LONG 3°11

LONG 3°11'58''

LONG 3°12'3''

LONG 3°12'14''

LONG 3°12'19''

LONG 3°12'22''

LONG 3°12'

LAT 55°57'9''

LAT 55°57'2''

metis   urban cartographies

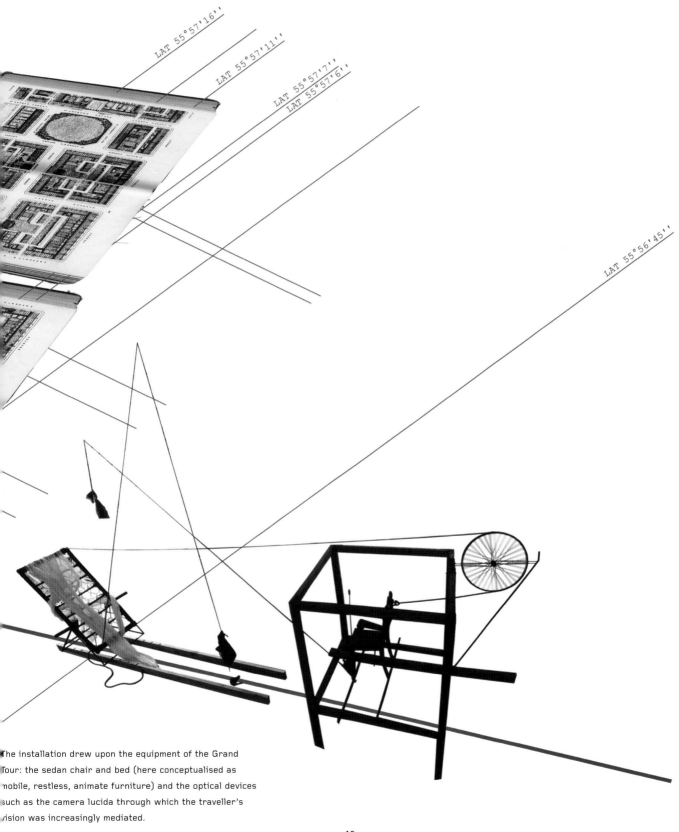

LAT 55°57'16''

LAT 55°57'11''

LAT 55°57'7''
LAT 55°57'6''

LAT 55°56'45''

The installation drew upon the equipment of the Grand
Tour: the sedan chair and bed (here conceptualised as
mobile, restless, animate furniture) and the optical devices
such as the camera lucida through which the traveller's
vision was increasingly mediated.

15

The absent body
of the traveller
forms the hinge
through which
the tremulous
furniture and
the measured,
cartographic
world beyond
the room
communicate.
The 'upright'
longitude is
related to the
posture of the
body in the
sedan chair
and the
'recumbent'
latitude to
the bed. The
resolution
between them
is the
mathematical
resolution of
the forces
through the
counterweight
mechanism, a
resolution that
is constantly
lost and
regained
as sand
gradually
slips between
the loose
weave in the
hessian sacks.

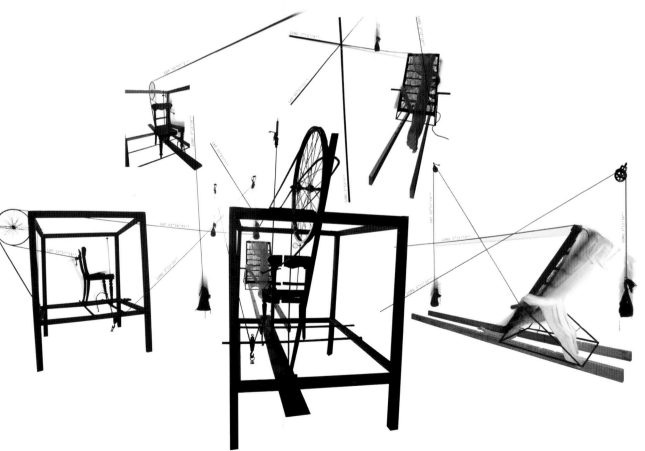

metis   latitude and longitude resolved

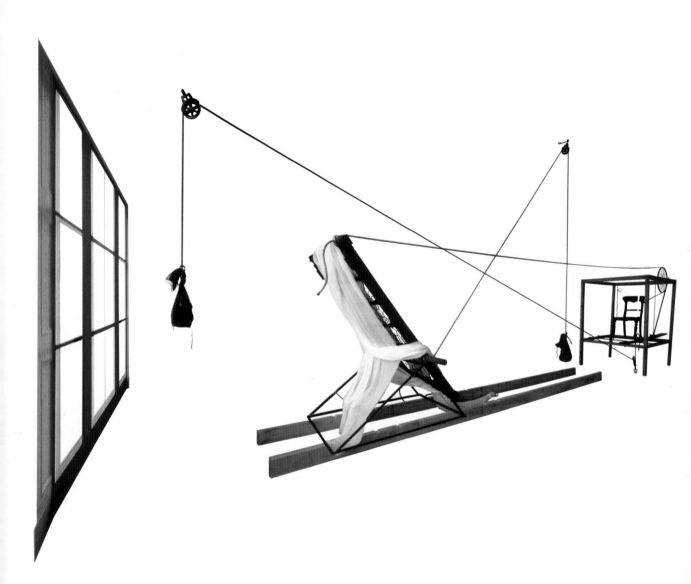

The entire assemblage constitutes a body: head, feet, flesh and sinews
are distributed within the room, which itself becomes a kind of sedan.
This figure gazes at the expanding landscape beyond, seen through
the grid of astragals — suggestive of lines of latitude and longitude —
upon the plane of the window. We imagined the Grand Tourist to be a
querulous character, impatiently stamping his foot.

metis

latitude and longitude resolved

metis

metis

urba

carto

Brita

metis

britannia basin housing

'Britannia Basin' is part of the extensive nineteenth-century industrial canal network of the northern English city of Manchester. This project developed as a critical response to a competition that sought proposals for housing adjacent to it that worked positively with architectural density, demonstrating how compelling and convivial spaces could be achieved on such 'brown field' sites (the now disused territories of the city that have historically been occupied by industry). Manufacturing and warehouse buildings typically define the scale of these areas.

Inherent within the brief was the desire for a strategy that could be peculiarly responsive to the specific demands and characteristics of the given site while, at the same time, acting as a prototype for future developments in similar areas.

A useful starting point seemed to be to conceptualise the architecture as an assemblage of various pieces which could move and take on differing relationships to one another in response to the particular qualities of a site. If one set of these was then conceived as th mobile, informal elements (that would seem closer in character to the scattered objects in the goods-yard or upon the canal-side than to the surrounding industrial architecture), another could be considered as the set which framed the first, tethering the elements in their specific locations.

Moving from site to site, the constellation described by the informal pieces would shift and thus the entire collection of architectural elements, like gaming-pieces, be constantly reconfigured as they encountered new terrains: the framing elements lifting, the lower pieces moving and then the framing elements descending again to fix them in a new pattern.

This thinking pointed to a kind of architecture that developed in sectional terms, evolving a stratification that moved from the subterranean to a 'ground level' datum, to the space of the informal elements, to the plane of the framing pieces. And this, in turn, opened the opportunity for an architecture which began, in the context of housing, to develop what each of these differing sectional 'worlds' might be.

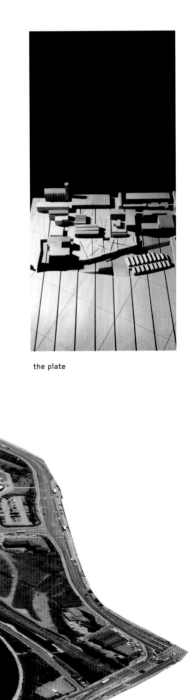

the plate

bridgewater
canal

metis

britannia basin

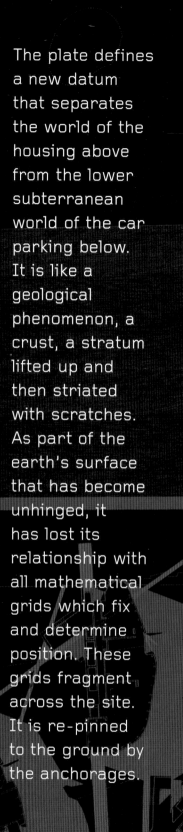

The plate defines
a new datum
that separates
the world of the
housing above
from the lower
subterranean
world of the car
parking below.
It is like a
geological
phenomenon, a
crust, a stratum
lifted up and
then striated
with scratches.
As part of the
earth's surface
that has become
unhinged, it
has lost its
relationship with
all mathematical
grids which fix
and determine
position. These
grids fragment
across the site.
It is re-pinned
to the ground by
the anchorages.

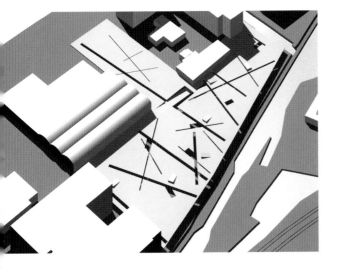

the plate

arkhive level plan

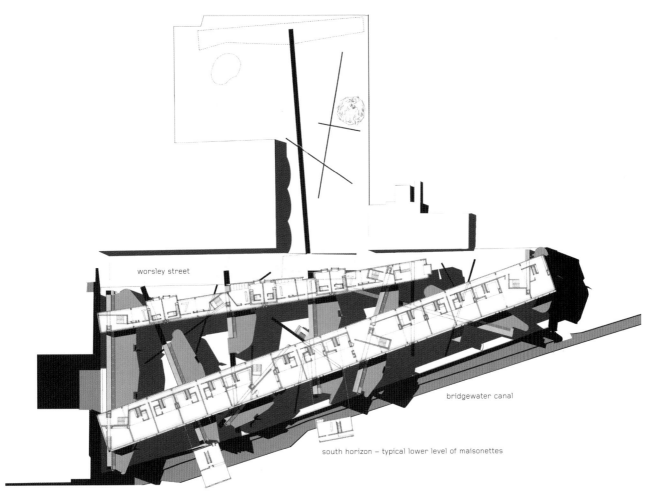

worsley street

bridgewater canal

south horizon – typical lower level of maisonettes

north horizon – typical upper level of maisonettes

horizon level plan

metis   britannia basin

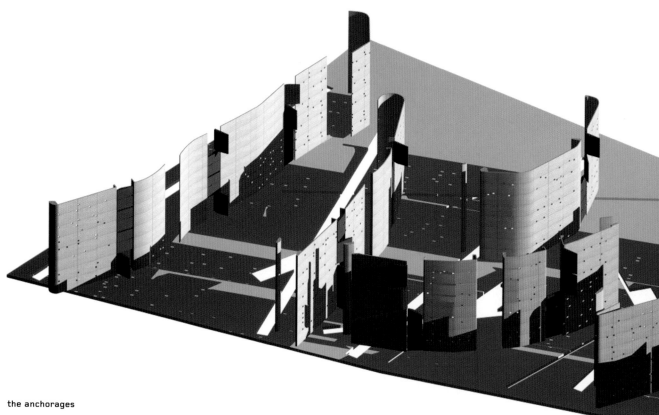

the anchorages

Spines, supports, places of enclosure, protection and
intimacy. Here the body is both exposed and enfolded:
cooking, washing, and defecation occur within them. The
anchorages are inscrutable concrete cases into and out of
which the body moves. The traces it leaves pass out of them
and into the world. As the anchorages locate the housing,
so too they maintain discrete points of connection between
the detached plate and the earth.

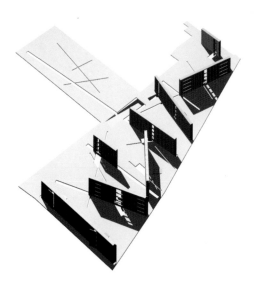

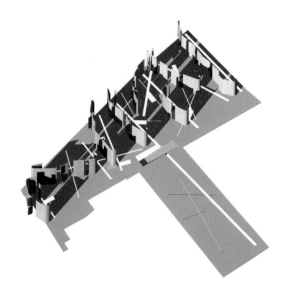

the anchorages

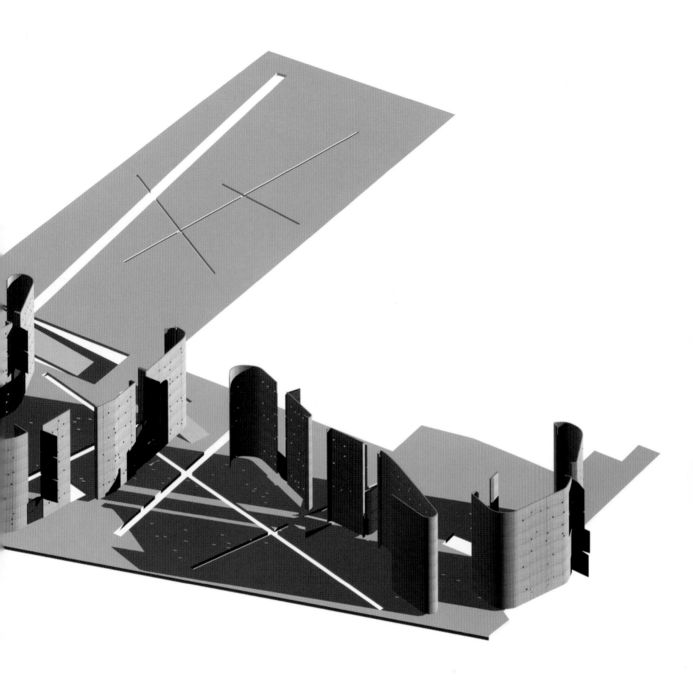

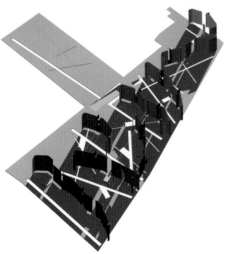

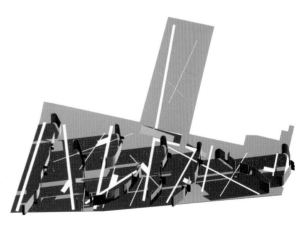

the arkhive skins

29

metis

britannia basin

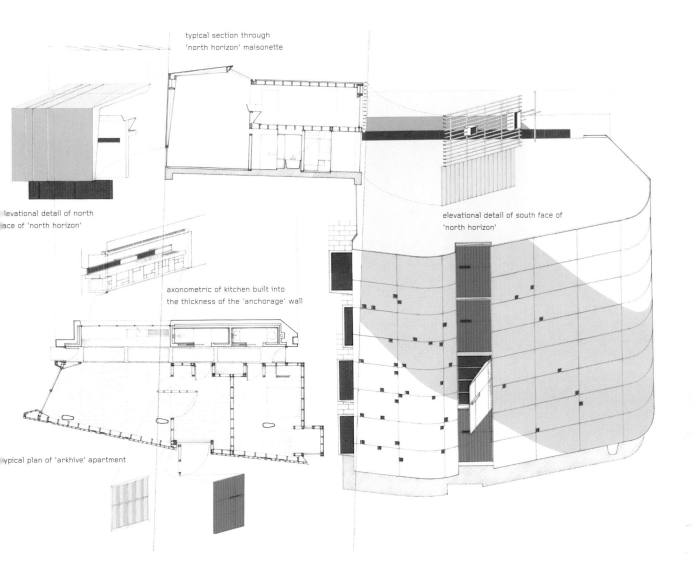

typical section through
'north horizon' maisonette

elevational detail of north
ace of 'north horizon'

elevational detail of south face of
'north horizon'

axonometric of kitchen built into
the thickness of the 'anchorage' wall

ypical plan of 'arkhive' apartment

the horizons

wo lines which descend upon and frame the arkhive housing,
uspending it between the lifted plate and the sky. Directional beams
vhich speak of the movement of the canal and of the railway. Lines
against which the movement of the sun is reckoned; lines over which it
ises and enters into the depths of the architecture below.

the arkhives

A kind of habitation which attaches to an already-given surface. Boat
and cabinet-like, they speak of movement, of other configurations, other
juxtapositions, other horizons. The temporality of the arkhives is that
of suspended movement; the paradox of the houseboat which, at its
moorings, outlasts everything that is around it. They float above the
surface of the plate and smell and sound of wood.

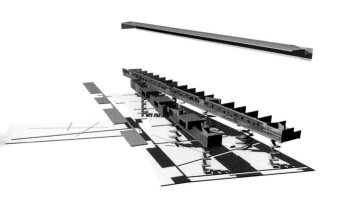

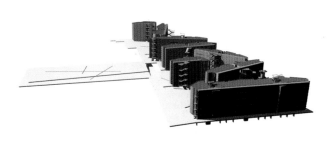

metis

britannia basin

metis

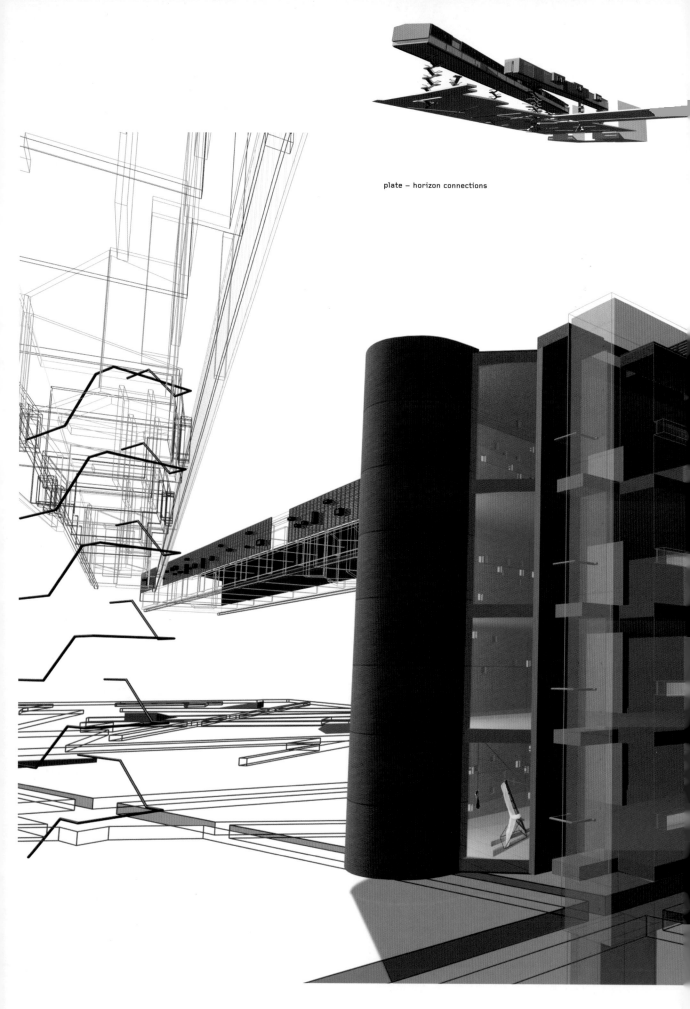

plate – horizon connections

metis   urban cartographies

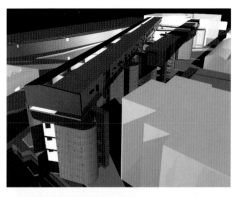

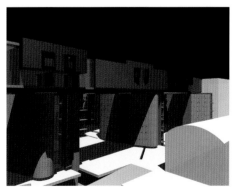

metis   britannia basin

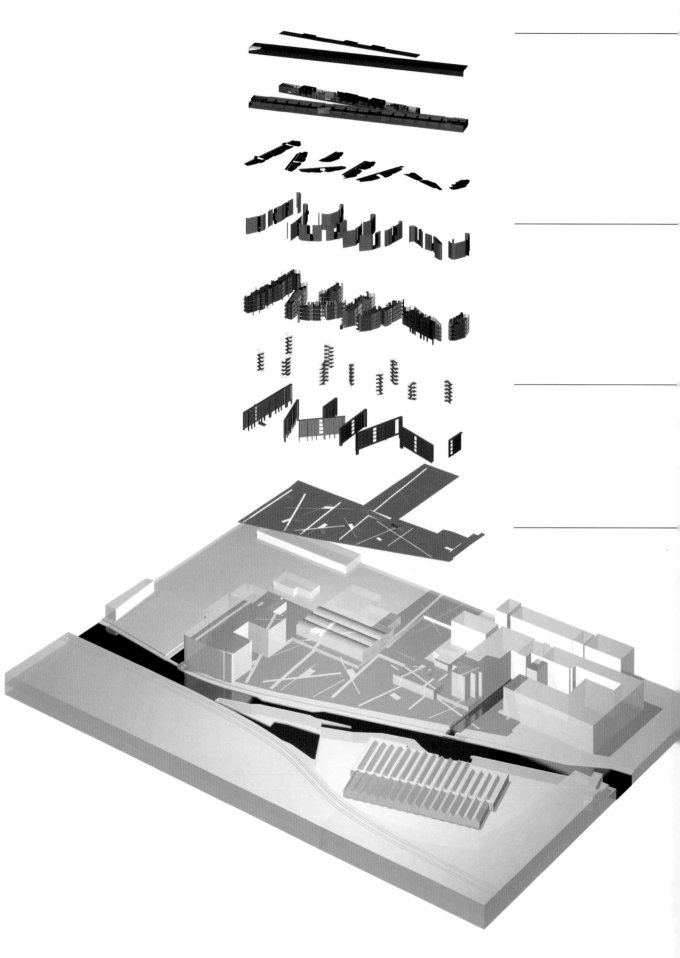

the horizons

Programme – Skyhouses. Mezzanine housing which is about the panorama of the surrounding city and the movements of the sky. The light in the apartments is luminous, nuanced and constantly changing. A 'mask', scored with thin channels of glazing, clads the north façade of the north horizon. The apartments in the south horizon face the sun while in the north horizon sunlight is drawn deep into the spaces by rooflight glazing. The horizons are accessed by lifts and stairs through certain of the anchorages.

Materials – Access routes are clad with luminescent industrial C-section glazing. Clear glazing to the south-facing façades is covered with a cedar brise-soleil. In the north horizon this is punctuated with deep box-windows formed from plywood and glass. The 'mask' to the north façade of the north horizon is clad with zinc.

the arkhives

Programme – The arkhives are directional housing; they look along the lines of the cuts and the anchorages. In the interiors, screens twist open, combining and enlarging spaces. The side walls are perforated with points of light.

Materials – Timber construction off concrete floors. Walls of rainscreen construction with plywood panels on the exterior. Into this is set a patterning of glass lenses. The shutters covering the large side windows are clad with cor-ten steel.

the anchorages

Programme – The anchorages are massive walls which hold kitchens, shower rooms, toilets and lifts for the housing. Starting at the car park, they pass through the slots cut into the plate and rise four storeys above plate level. They give access from the car park and the surface of the plate, via the lifts and staircases which they support, to the arkhive and the horizon housing above. They are the structural supports to which the arkhive and horizon housing attach.

Material – In-situ concrete on the exterior surfaces and pre-cast concrete on the interior.

the plate

Programme – Below the plate is the car park which is entered from Worsley Street. It is lit from the canal edge (which is left open) and is punctuated by shards of light which pass through the slots incised within the plate. The surface of the plate is an urban public space; the apartments can be accessed directly from it and from the car park below. The cuts in the plate south of Worsley Street begin, as they break into the soil, to describe a garden area.

Materials – Concrete, with metal grilles covering the exposed slots.

metis   britannia basin

metis

urba

carto

Mime

industrial archaeology and the future of the city: project for the ex-magazzini generali area of Verona, Italy

In the early 1900s a major urban agglomeration developed to the south of Verona, beyond the walls of the old city. The industrial base for this growth was the processing and distribution of agricultural produce from the city's hinterland. The expansion was focused on the area around the extraordinary sequence of warehouse buildings and extensive rail yards which served this industry. The most striking of these was a huge, refrigerated rotunda: within it laden rail carriages were rotated on a central turn-table before being docked and stored in the segments of the drum.

The project presents a new urban proposal for the rail yards and warehouses which now lie derelict. As well as responding to demands for facilities for the Verona Fair (whose principal buildings lie across the Viale del Lavoro from the warehouse zone), the project provides a series of park and civic spaces and services currently lacking from Verona South.

Taking the idea of Verona South as a kind of extra-mural 'double' of the old walled city, a set of four mimetic urban strategies were developed which worked with the transformative potential of the copy. The mimetic processes iterate between the source and the new condition with the 'animation frames' describing stages in the iterative progression. Already, when one looks at the urban plan of Verona, one has a strange intimation of this process, the rotunda of the Magazzani Generali resonating with the Roman amphitheatre at the end of the long axis defined by the road leading into the ancient city.

This project takes elements in the existing urban texture (the warehouses, church, rail lines, etc.) and resituates them: using the mimetic strategies it draws them into a new configuration by working upon and shifting the contextual ground within which they are embedded.

metis   mimetic urbanism

unfolding – enfolding

From an analysis of the morphology of the city wall of Verona, a wall, whose rules are set by the analysis, is woven through the site. It links, cradles, and enfolds existing structures and, through its convolutions, constructs new accommodation.

drift – anchorage

The rail lines in the southern part of the decommissioned zone become the cue for a series of walls which structure a new culture-park, a complex of garden strips which, when taken with the garden areas formed to the east of the 'wall' on the Magazzini Generali site, represents a major new complex of green spaces. Through the strips and garden territories flows a series of buildings: driftworks.

42

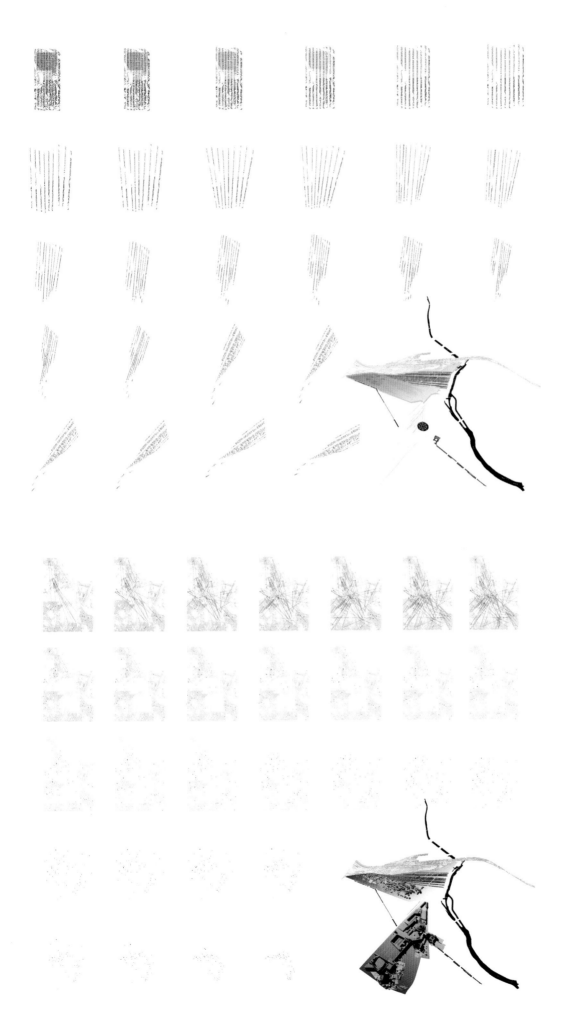

excavation – sedimentation

The Renaissance city is divided into strips calibrated by the divisions of the Roman city. These strips are then used to construct a new complex on the northern area of the decommissioned railtrack zone. The process is one of excavation and sedimentation, the new programmes being laid in to the earth.

constellation – settlement

A constellation of houses is selected from the 'other city' of Verona South and then, based upon their orientation, projected onto the site to form a texture of small residential, commercial, and cultural programmes.

metis

mimetic urbanism

the mimetic assemblage

in the city

programmatic distribution

cultural

– church
– galleries
– theatres
– auditoria
– libraries
– museums
– sports facilities

driftworks

– galleries
– performance spaces
– music conservatories
– greenhouses
– booksellers
– restaurants and cafés
– exhibition rooms

commercial

– retail
– offices
– studios
– workshops
– hotels

facilities for the 'Verona Fair'

– auditoria
– performance spaces
– lecture halls
– exhibition concourses
– meeting rooms
– administration

projected houses

– the sounding house
– the house of the merchant
– the house of wood
– the summer house
– the musician's house
– the abandoned house
– the house of rain
– the compass house
– the boat house
– the collapsed house

gardens/green areas/landscape connections

– botanic gardens in sedimented strip
– culture park with patterning of small garden territories
– major urban 'walled garden'

roads and parking

– level of highway along Viale del Lavoro dropped below grade
– new underground parking in proximity to Verona Fair complex
– closure or reduction to service status of roads crossing the site
– new link road to north west

water and walks

– pedestrian link along reopened canal, passing beside the church of Santa Teresa and running on toward the Adige river
– new pedestrian route northward along the line of Viale del Lavoro toward the city centre
– bridges crossing the sedimented strips

lines of projection

lines of projection

lines of projection

lines of projection

metis

urban cartographies

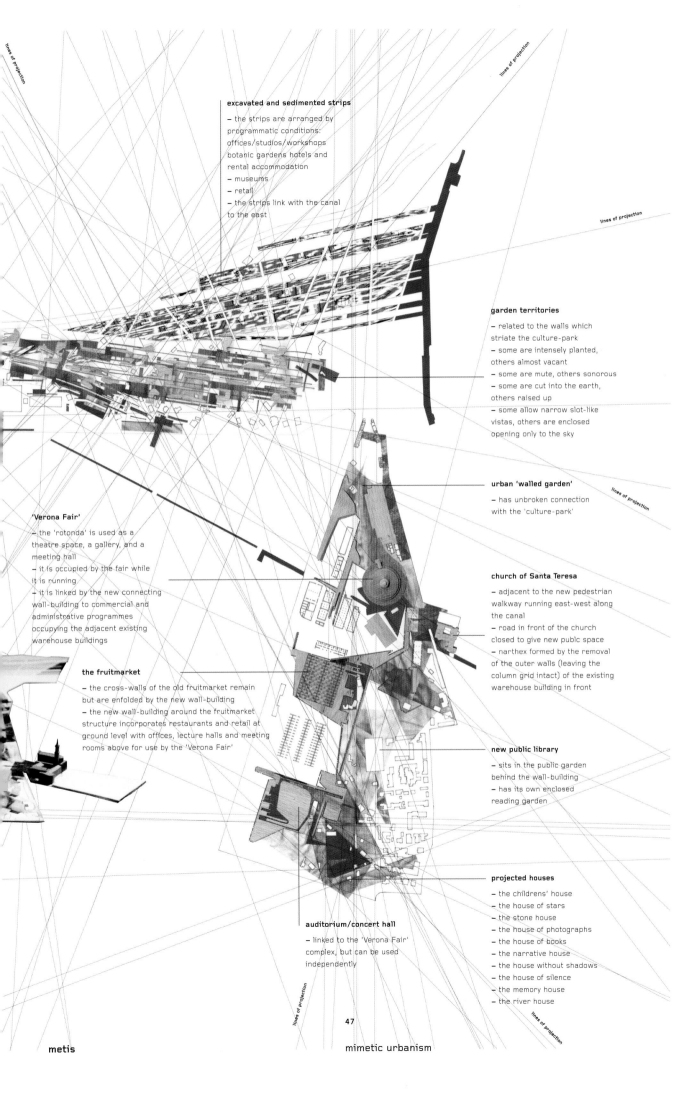

excavated and sedimented strips

– the strips are arranged by programmatic conditions:
offices/studios/workshops
botanic gardens hotels and rental accommodation
– museums
– retail
– the strips link with the canal to the east

garden territories

– related to the walls which striate the culture-park
– some are intensely planted, others almost vacant
– some are mute, others sonorous
– some are cut into the earth, others raised up
– some allow narrow slot-like vistas, others are enclosed opening only to the sky

urban 'walled garden'

– has unbroken connection with the 'culture-park'

'Verona Fair'

– the 'rotonda' is used as a theatre space, a gallery, and a meeting hall
– it is occupied by the fair while it is running
– it is linked by the new connecting wall-building to commercial and administrative programmes occupying the adjacent existing warehouse buildings

church of Santa Teresa

– adjacent to the new pedestrian walkway running east-west along the canal
– road in front of the church closed to give new publc space
– narthex formed by the removal of the outer walls (leaving the column grid intact) of the existing warehouse building in front

the fruitmarket

– the cross-walls of the old fruitmarket remain but are enfolded by the new wall-building
– the new wall-building around the fruitmarket structure incorporates restaurants and retail at ground level with offices, lecture halls and meeting rooms above for use by the 'Verona Fair'

new public library

– sits in the public garden behind the wall-building
– has its own enclosed reading garden

projected houses

– the childrens' house
– the house of stars
– the stone house
– the house of photographs
– the house of books
– the narrative house
– the house without shadows
– the house of silence
– the memory house
– the river house

auditorium/concert hall

– linked to the 'Verona Fair' complex, but can be used independently

lines of projection

metis   mimetic urbanism

metis

urba

carto

Micr

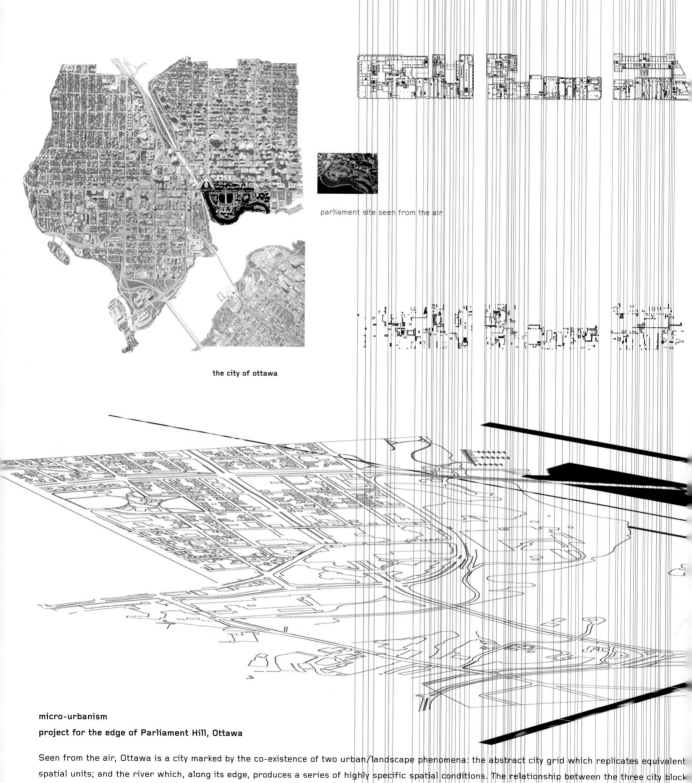

parliament site seen from the air

the city of ottawa

micro-urbanism

project for the edge of Parliament Hill, Ottawa

Seen from the air, Ottawa is a city marked by the co-existence of two urban/landscape phenomena: the abstract city grid which replicates equivalent spatial units; and the river which, along its edge, produces a series of highly specific spatial conditions. The relationship between the three city blocks of the site and the parliamentary buildings that they face is grounded in this broader duality. The parliamentary buildings are highly figurative: before them the weave of the city grid is laid out like a textile.

This project is concerned with developing a large urban site that forms the southern edge of Parliament Hill. It is a hybrid programmatic proposal which incorporates cultural and governmental facilities.

50

metis

urban cartographies

The architectural strategy for the proposal developed from the notion that the city (and, by extension, the land beyond) might in some way be gathered up or folded into the site (with all the density that the metaphor implies) and thus brought into a relationship with the parliamentary complex. Through the topology of the folds a new urban continuum would be established, drawing together the space of the parliament and the space of the city.

Although the scheme envisages removing the existing buildings from the site, it retains the grain of the lot lines which striate the territory and which project outward, structuring the fabric of the city. Furthermore, the building pattern across the site is 'edited', a procedure which breaks down the cellular nature of the existing morphology, to produce a notional texture of minor architectural elements which can then be reinscribed within the new structure.

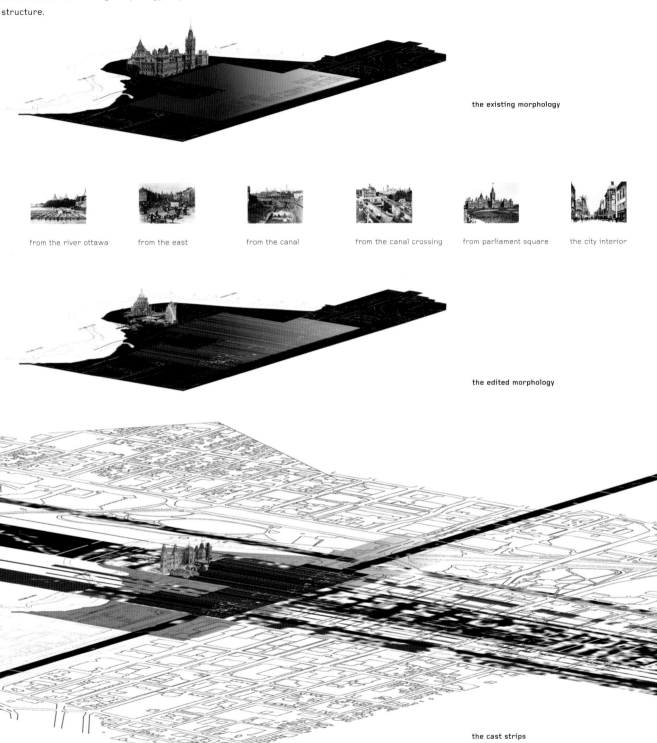

the existing morphology

from the river ottawa   from the east   from the canal   from the canal crossing   from parliament square   the city interior

the edited morphology

the cast strips

metis   micro urbanism

The extension of the lot lines beyond the site suggested a
reading of them as a series of journeys from the site into
the city. The lines were identified through reference to a
selection of appropriated urban narratives. These
narratives were analysed to produce a series of defining
structural meta-texts.

metis

urban cartographies

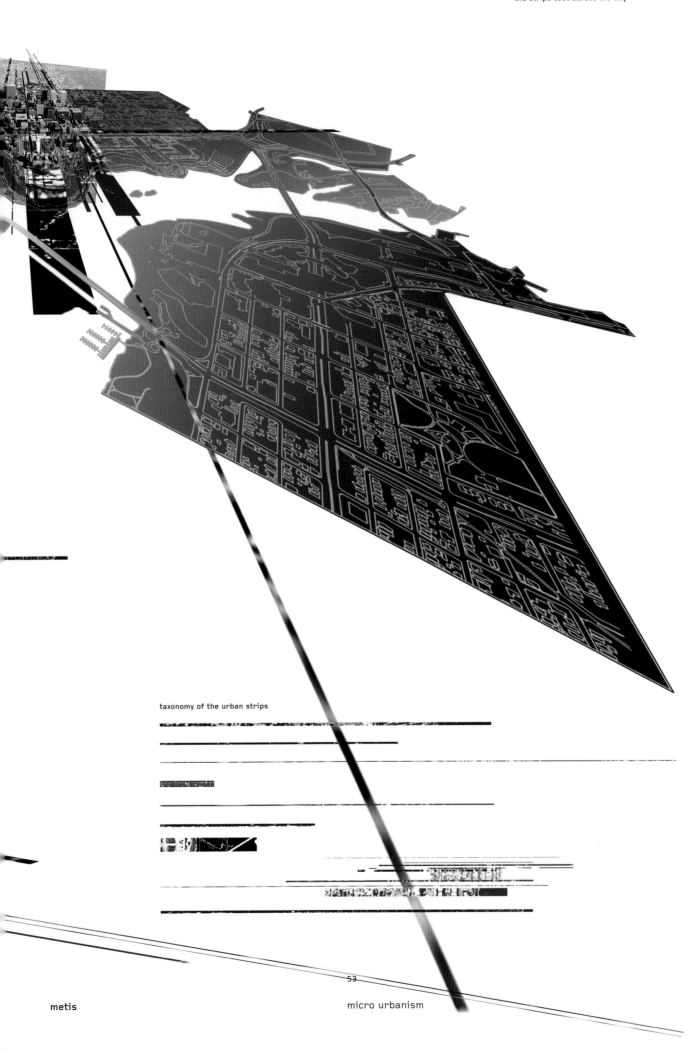

taxonomy of the urban strips

metis   micro urbanism

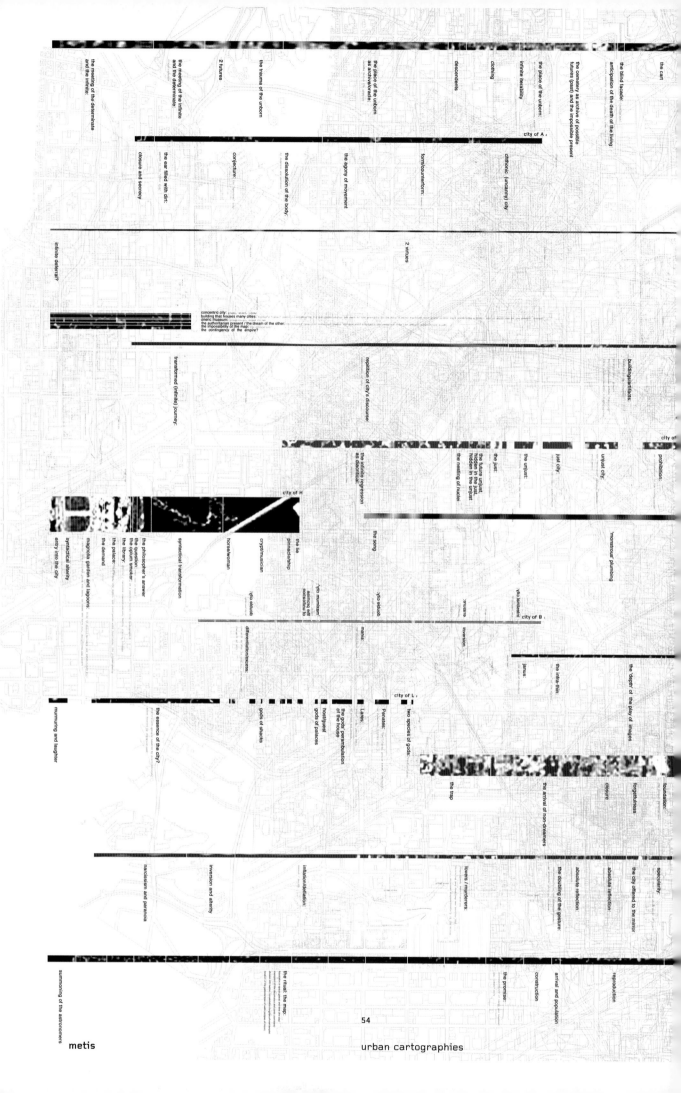

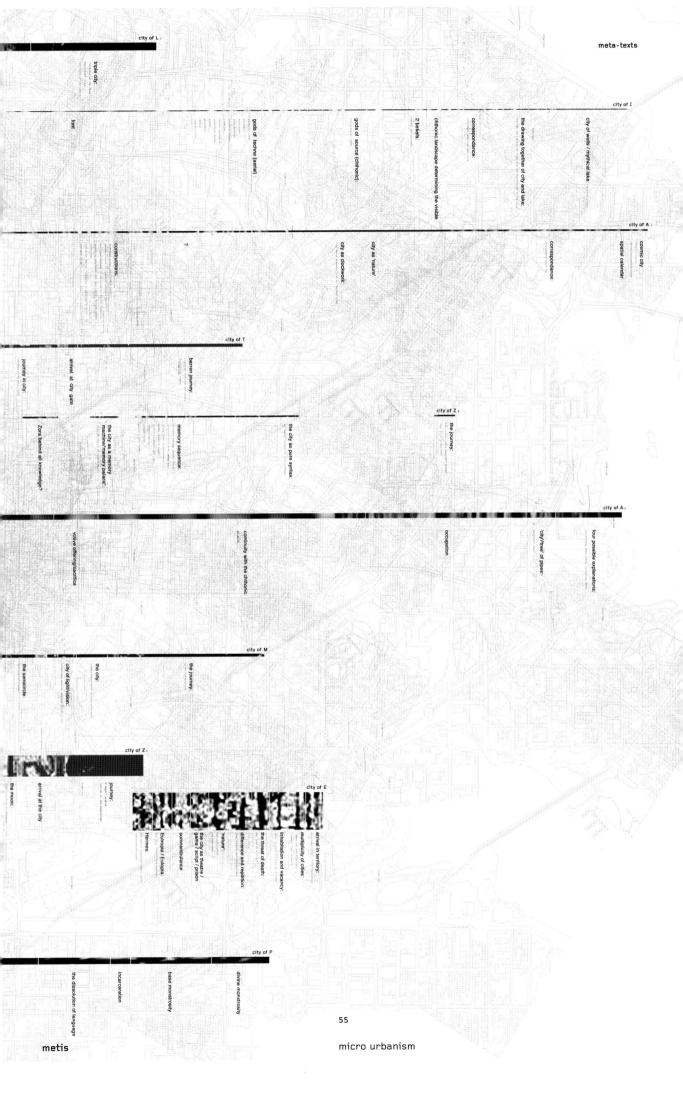

city of L

triple city

font

city of I

gods of techne (aerial):

gods of source (chthonic):

chthonic landscape determining the visible

2 beliefs:

correspondance:

the drawing together of city and lake:

city of wells / mythical lake

city of A

cosmic city

spatial calendar

correspondance:

constructions:

?

city as 'nature'

city as clockwork:

city of T

journey in city:

arrival at city gate

barren journey:

memory sequence:

the city as a memory machine/ memory palace:

the city as pure syntax:

city of Z

the journey:

Zora behind all knowledge?

city of A

votive offering/sacrifice

continuity with the chthonic:

occupation

'city/tree' of pipes:

four possible explanations:

city of M

the semicircle:

city of light/vision:

the city:

the journey:

city of Z

the moon:

arrival at the city

journey:

Hermes:

Eutropia / Eutopia

somnambulance

the city as theatre / game / script / prison

'nature':

difference and repitition:

the threat of death:

inhabitation and vacancy:

multiplicity of cities:

arrival in territory:

city of E

city of P

divine monstrosity

base monstrosity

incarceration

the dissolution of language

metis

micro urbanism

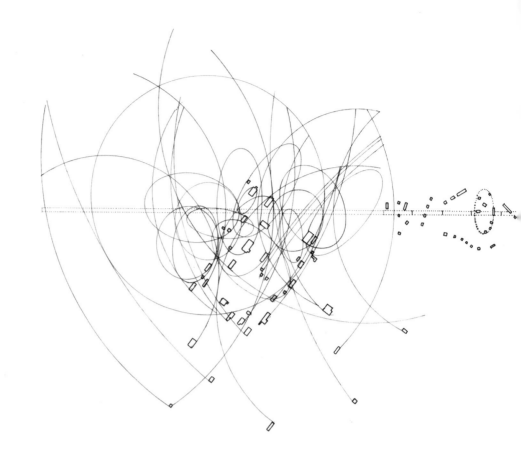

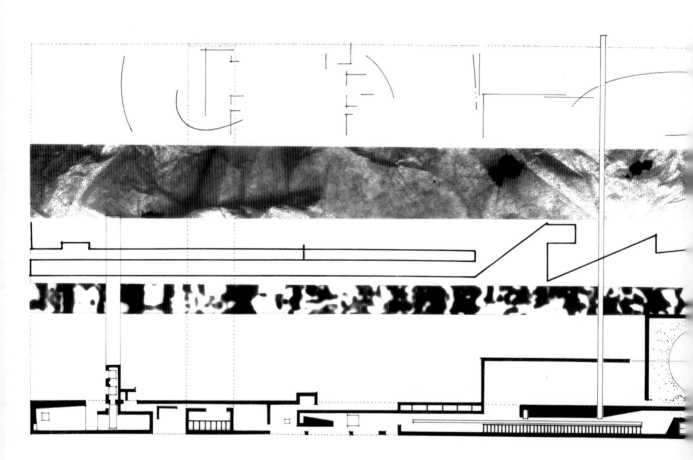

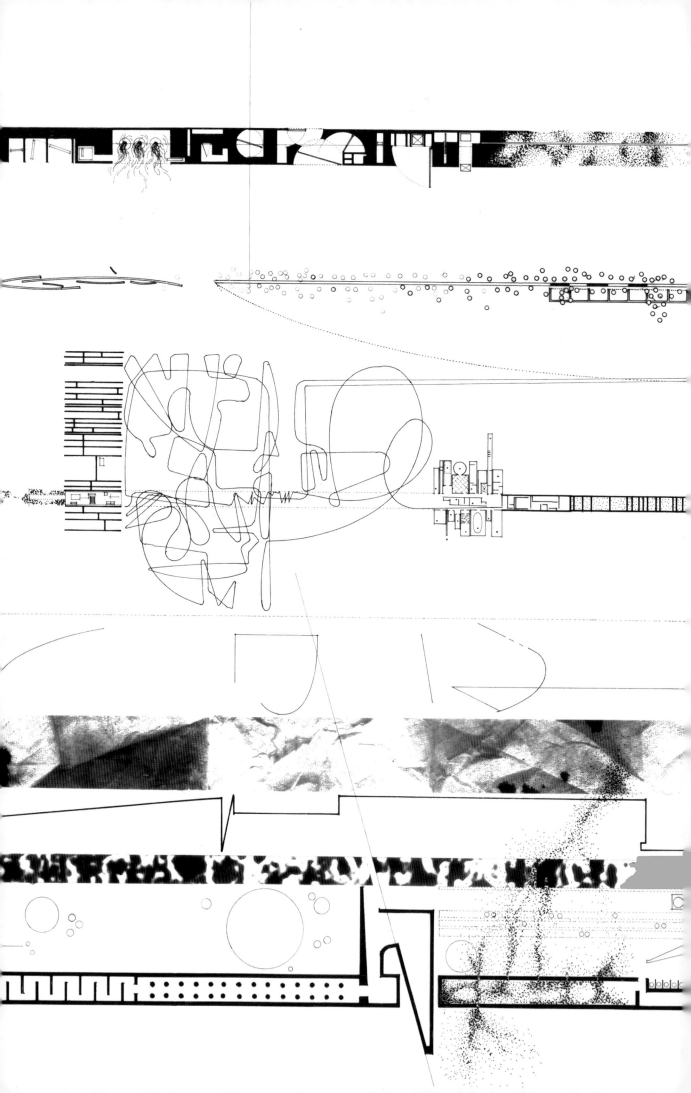

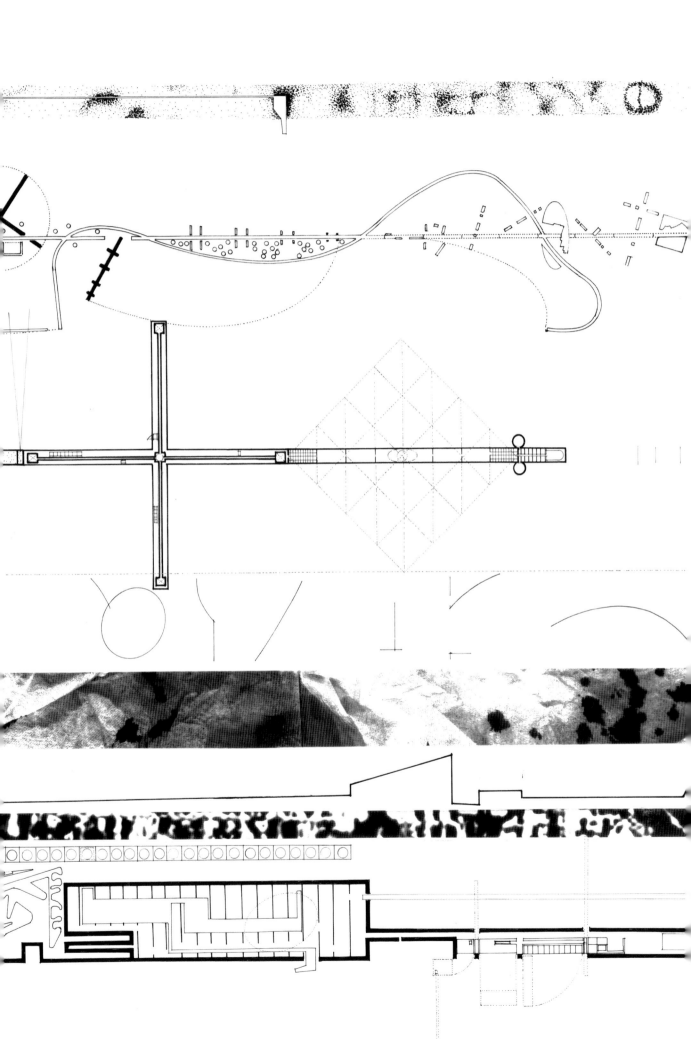

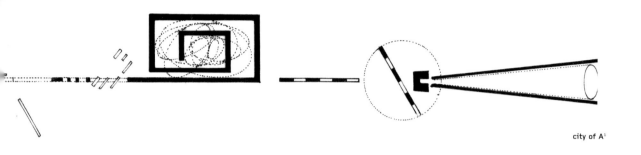

city of A¹

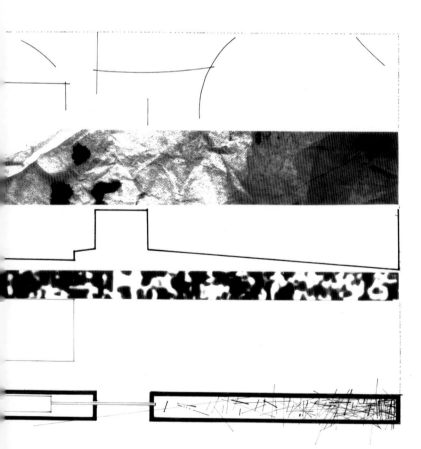

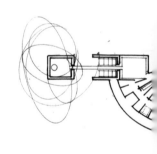

city of F

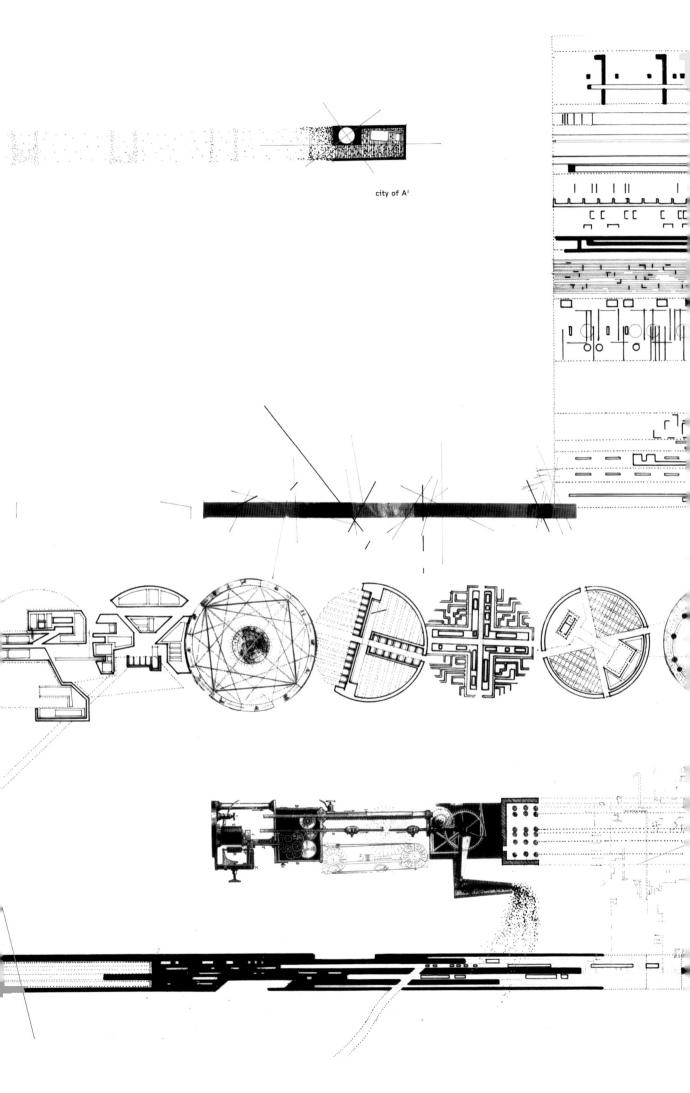

city of A²

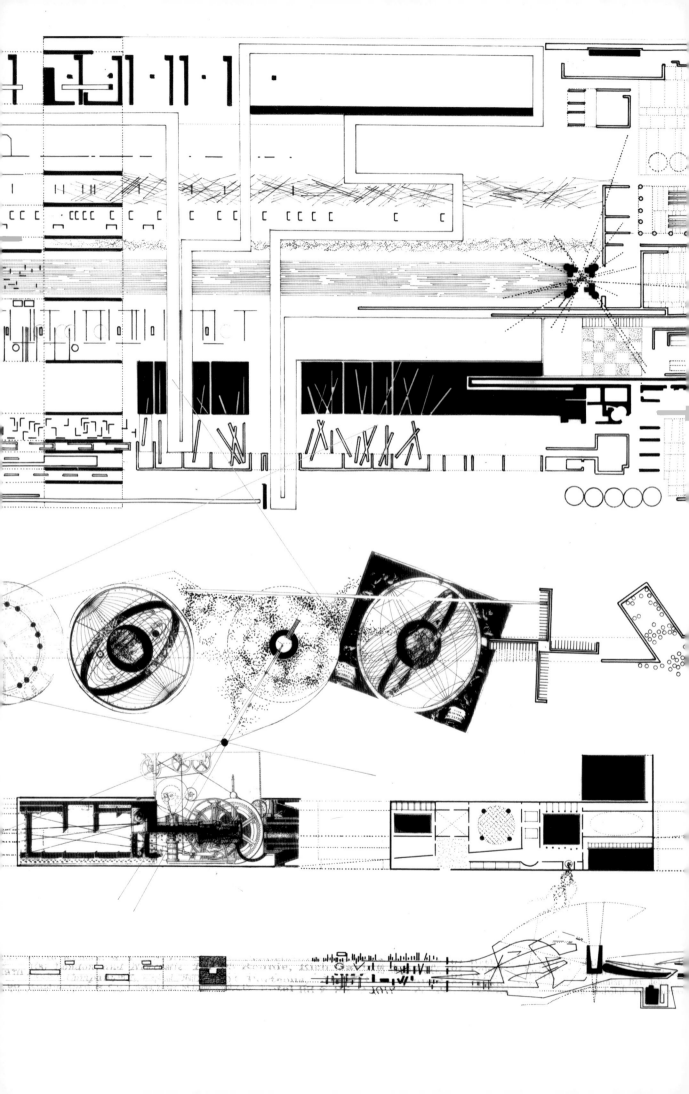

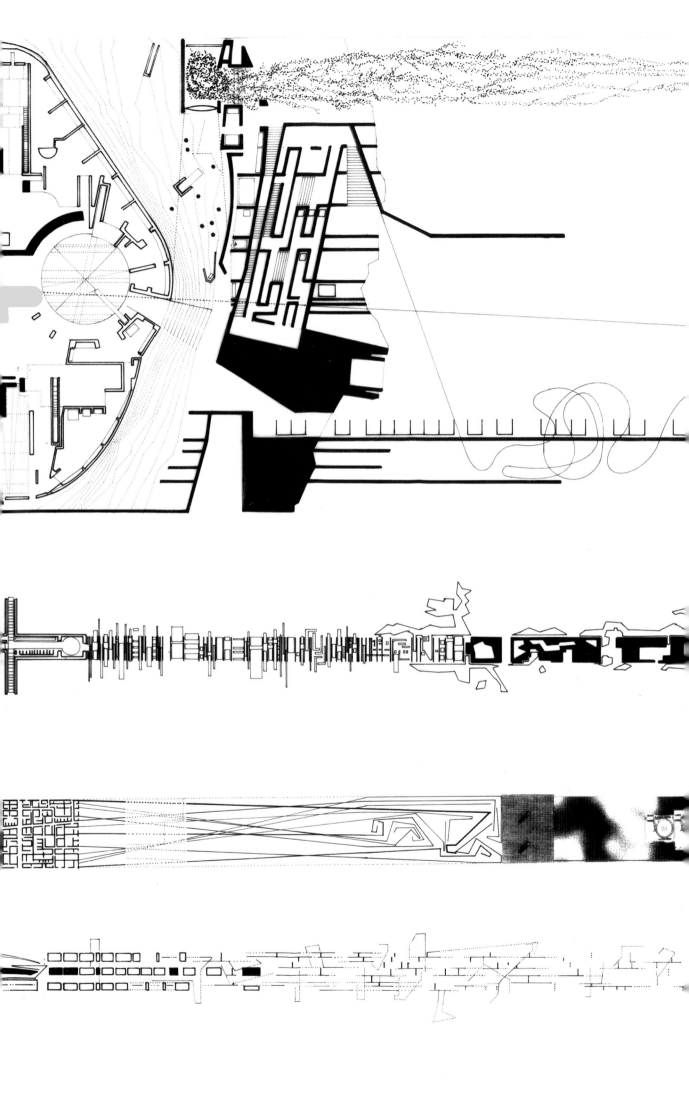

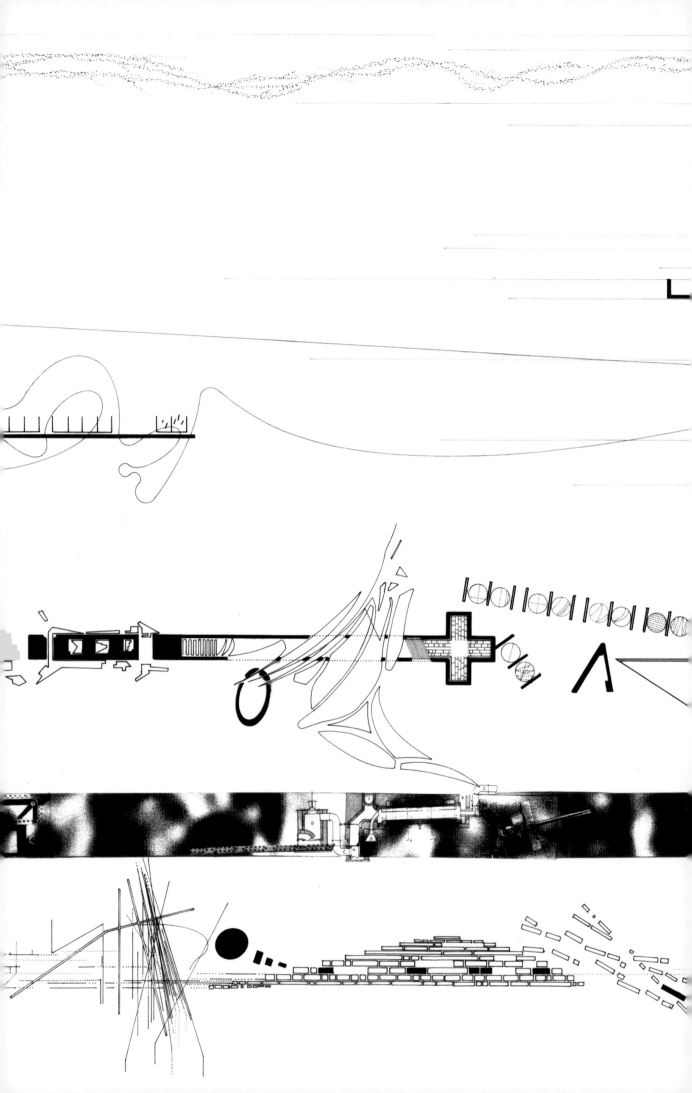

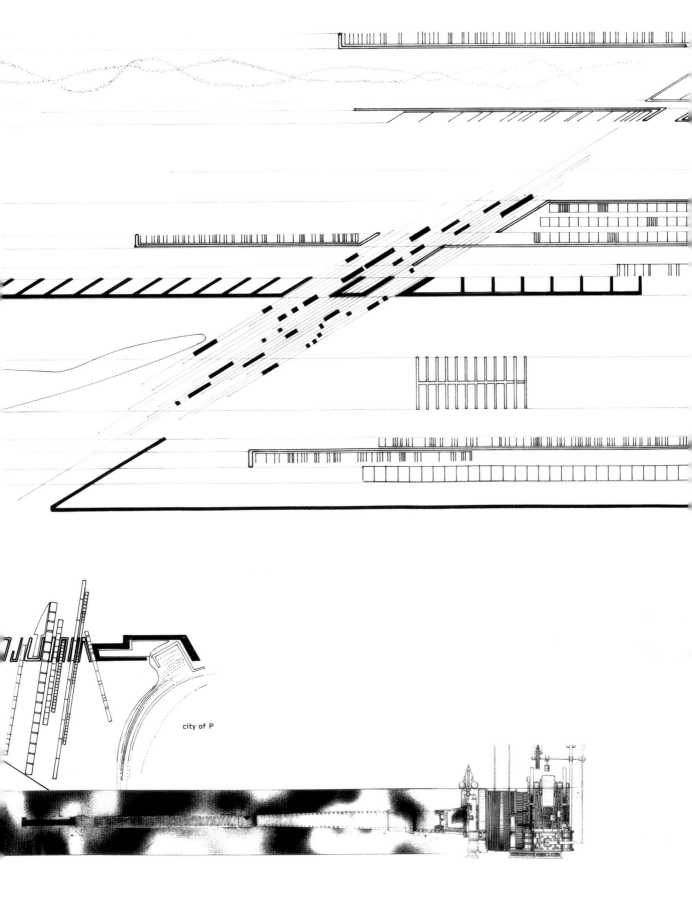

city of P

city of B[2]

city of L[1]

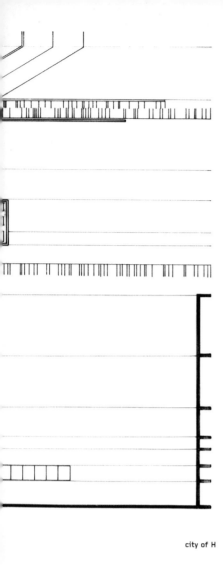

city of H

The narratives and meta-texts, read against the fabric of the city, were used to elaborate a series of narrative architectural strips. The reach of the strips, which vary widely, was suggested by the interplay of the text and the representations of the city deployed. Some are highly extensive: A^1, for example, traverses the city. Others are more compressed: H undertakes an intricate exploration and reperformance of the spaces of the central parliamentary building itself.

Although the strips vary in scale when sited in the city, the drawing for each was performed at a common physical length. The consequence of this was that when the strips were reintegrated into the city by scaling, a series of architectural effects operating at differing scales and densities was produced.

taxonomy of the narrative strips

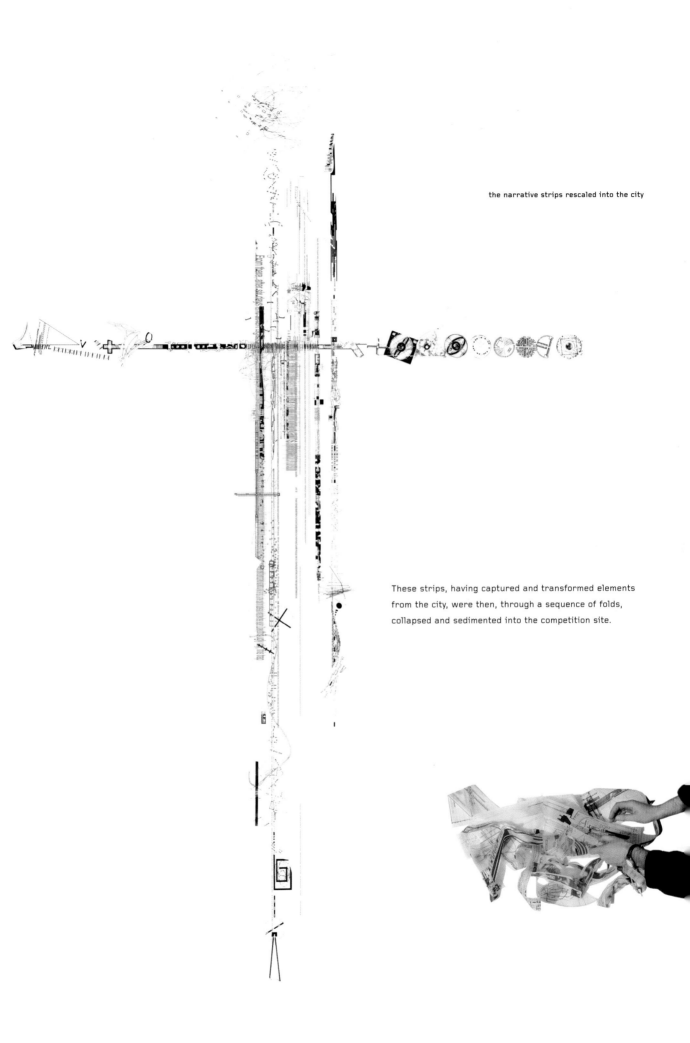

the narrative strips rescaled into the city

These strips, having captured and transformed elements
from the city, were then, through a sequence of folds,
collapsed and sedimented into the competition site.

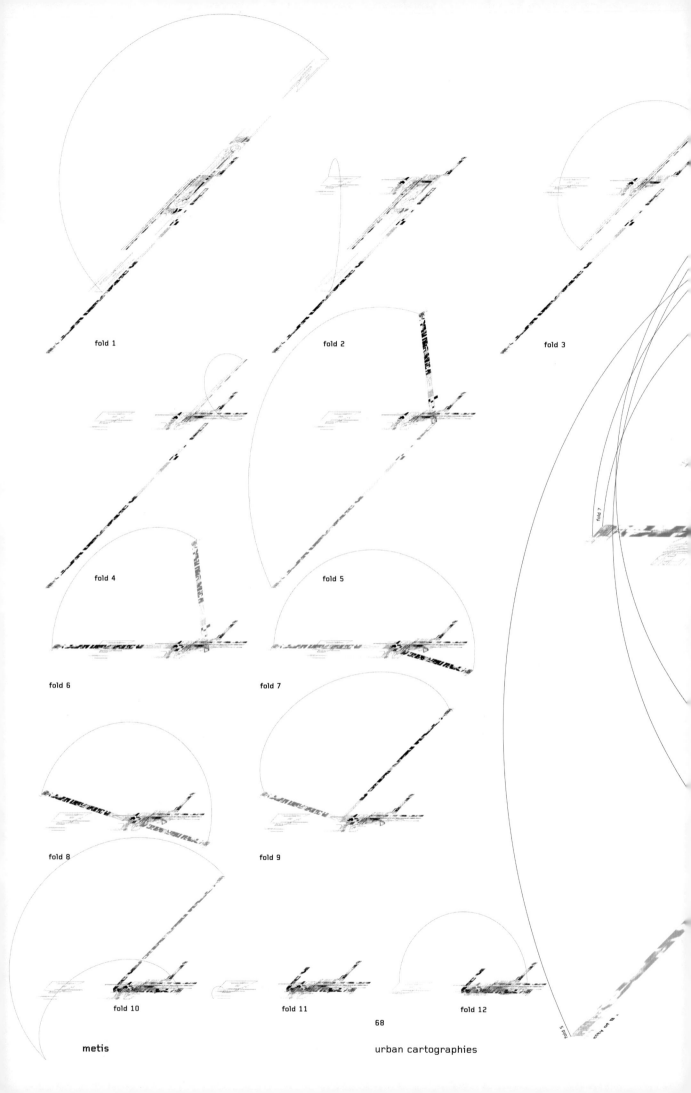

fold 1

fold 2

fold 3

fold 4

fold 5

fold 6

fold 7

fold 8

fold 9

fold 10

fold 11

fold 12

metis

urban cartographies

sequence of folds

city of B¹
city of F
city of H

city of B² – the knot

fold 13

fold 14

fold 15

fold 16

metis   micro urbanism

site plan

basement mezzanine plan (+73m)

metis   urban cartographies

section

ground level plan (+79m)

metis

micro urbanism

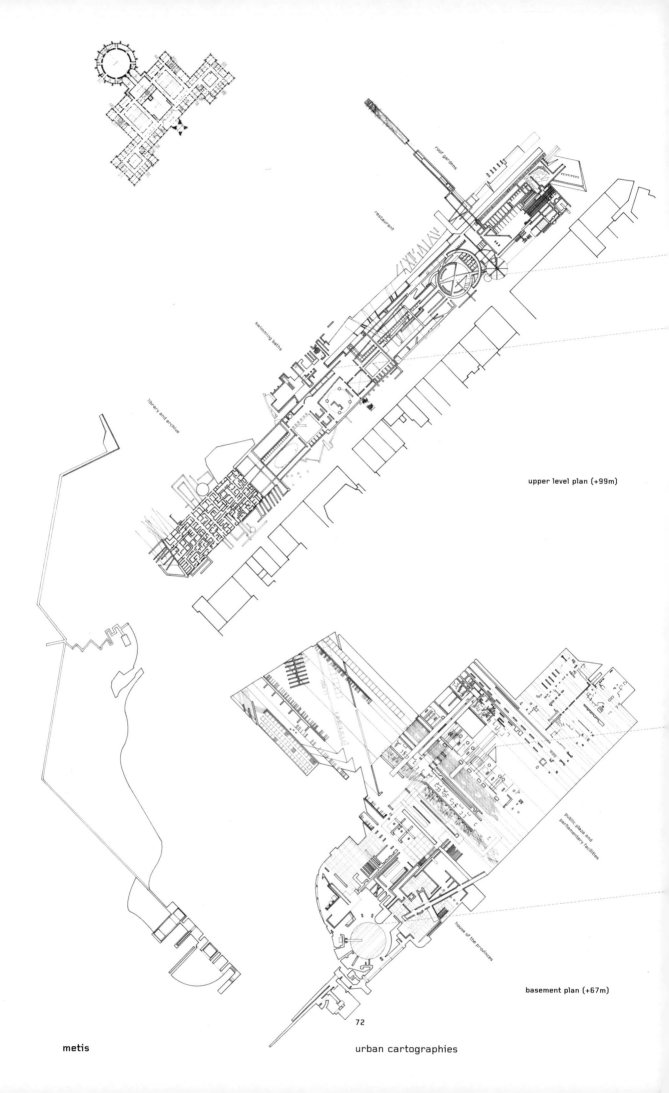

roof gardens

restaurant

swimming baths

library and archive

upper level plan (+99m)

public plaza and
parliamentary facilities

house of the provinces

basement plan (+67m)

metis   urban cartographies

fold sedimentation

metis

micro urbanism

metis

urba

carto

Cabi

Latitude and Longitude Resolved
Britannia Basin – Manchester
Mimetic Urbanism – Verona
Micro Urbanism – Ottawa
Cabinet of the City – Rome

metis   urban cartographies

the cabinet of the city

gallery of modern and contemporary art, rome

To the north of the Porta Pia in Rome lie the buildings of the former Birra Peroni brewery. This project was developed to a brief which called for the reworking of a derelict group of buildings which had acted as stables and stores for the old brewery. Some refurbishment of the part fronting onto via Reggio Emilia had already taken place and this was to be incorporated into the new scheme. The redeveloped block was to house the municipal gallery of modern and contemporary art collections in Rome.

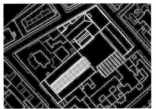

the space of the cabinet

The dimensions of the cabinet were imagined as being defined by the space of the glazed gallery between the two buildings facing via Reggio Emilia. The design process would develop by the emergence of this cabinet into the courtyard to the north-east of the gallery and its unfolding in stages to construct new connections with the existing structures and new accommodation of varying scales.

the axis

The cabinet's relation to the city was informed by the orientation of the glazed gallery between the two former stable buildings of the old brewery. The line of the gallery was projected as a notional sectional cut running through the fabric of Rome.

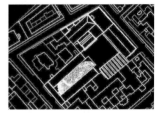

the urban field

The points where the sectional cut passed across the walls of Rome were used to limit the length of the line. This dimension was then referred to the proportions of the space of the glazed gallery on the competition site. Through this process an urban field existing within the walls of the city was defined and appropriated.

the cabinet of the city

The urban field was rescaled, and nested into the competition site. The seams, buildings and events represented upon it would later form the poetic and operational basis for both the constitution of the cabinet and its systematic and progressive unfolding into the site.

77

metis

cabinet of the city

the unfolding process

The opening of the cabinet was played as a kind of game. Its sequential movements produced a choreography that both constructed spaces in its own right and, by turns, implicated the spaces of the surrounding structures and the streets.

A poetics of folding, hinging, sliding and incising was elaborated. Through its hinged movement the river, for example, shifted to become a tall inhabitable exhibition case and a major element on the 'art trail'. Again, the sliding out of a 'drawer' from the extended cabinet of the city was used to define a public route which, passing over the event-space, connected the foyer with the bookshop, café and restaurant areas.

As the cabinet moved across the site, its sequential traces and the lines and arcs of its drawers and hinges incised the territory over which it passed, engaging with its depths. The topography of the courtyard and the complex chthonic landscape of the event-space below were informed by the rich and shadowed density of these marks.

The nearby catacombs were an important sectional datum and point of reference in thinking about the ways in which the project might articulate with the city's substratum.

nolli / photo cabinet

movement traces

dispersion of pieces

metis   cabinet of the city

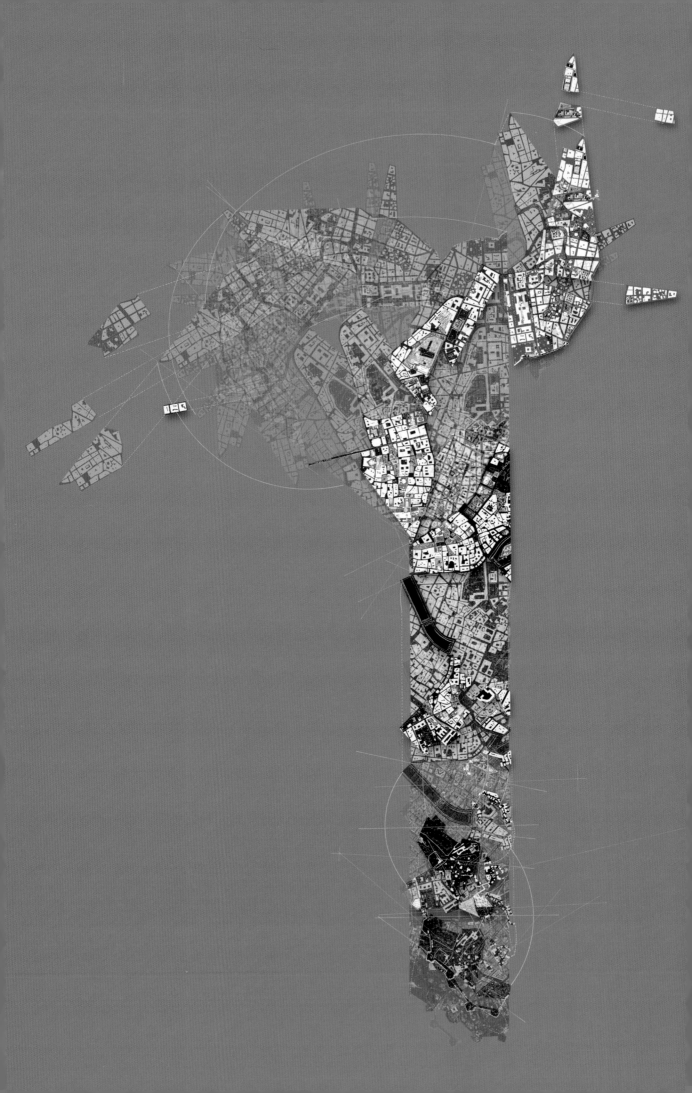

the closed cabinet

the opened cabinet

concept

One of the most intriguing manifestations of the princely and scholarly 'cultures of collecting' in early modern Europe were the famous cabinets which held wonders of art and nature. In the sixteenth and seventeenth centuries these fabulous collections were widespread both in Italy and beyond. The celebrated Kunstschrank which was given by the city of Augsburg to the king of Sweden in 1632 epitomised these cabinets at a compact scale. "Constructed of oak and ebony, the cabinet was richly inlaid with medallions of Limoges enamel, beaten silver, marble, agate, lapis lazuli, and intarsia panels of multicoloured woods, and crowned with a mound of crystals, corals, and shells surrounding a goblet fashioned from a Seychelles nut chased in gold and ornamented with the figures of Neptune and Thetis. Its secret compartments and drawers opened by means of hidden latches to reveal cunningly wrought artificialia and naturalia, including an anamorphic painting, an Italian spinet that played three tunes by an automatic mechanism, a pitcher made out of a nautilus shell worked with gilded silver, mathematical instruments, and a mummified monkey's claw. Laboriously assembled by master craftsmen over a period of six years, the cabinet not only housed in its recesses but also embodied in its design wonders of both art and nature" (Daston, Lorraine and Katherine Park, *Wonders and the Order of Nature, 1150-1750*, New York: Zone Books, 1998, p. 255.)

The design process from which the project evolved was grounded in an initial idea: that the new intervention be considered as a cabinet of collections housed within the existing structures on the site. Moreover, given the special geographical, institutional, and intellectual relationship that the gallery has with Rome, the architecture of the cabinet would be informed by the structure of the city. Aspects of the city would come to be embodied within the cabinet, this transaction between scales inviting two contrasting ideas: that Rome has, through the cabinet, become an object within the collection; and that the city itself be considered, in its unparalleled historical complexity and stratification, as an extraordinary cabinet of collections within which the site is held.

metis

cabinet of the city

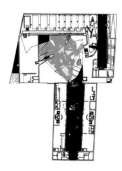

access and response to streets

The courtyard/garden level of the scheme is conceived as a topography that is continuous with the streets beyond. Pedestrian access to the site occurs in three locations: at via Reggio Emilia (between the two former stables buildings); at via Nizza; and at via Cagliari. The design allows 24-hour access to the courtyard/garden entering and exiting at these locations. The site becomes part of the gradated public routes of the city, and the gallery's exhibitions participate in its life. At via Nizza, the entrance sequence begins by filtering through the facade of the existing building. The choice is then either to enter the foyer or else to ascend the ramping ground plane to the left leading to courtyard/ garden level. The entrance at via Cagliari leads the visitor through the facade of the existing building, allowing views to the right down into the exhibition space. The visitor arrives between the café/restaurant and the bookshop and also finds here an information point for the 'art trail'. Access to the main foyer across the site can be gained through the courtyard/garden or by the 'beam' which crosses above the event-space and is accessed by the secondary foyer adjacent to the public multi-media resource (below the bookshop).

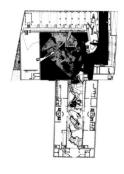

garden/open spaces/topography

The public exterior spaces of the project form an unbroken incised and folded surface which is understood as part of the landscape of the city. Someone moving through these spaces encounters a sequence of events constructed through the unfolding process. They are constantly aware of the depths of the site, of the comple topography of the event-space situated below, and sometimes seen through, the incised ground surface. Entry at via Reggio Emilia takes the visitor around the top of a sunken sculpture court before leading on past a series of exhibition structures defined by the unfolded cabinet. Various strategies of display encourage engagement with the fabric of the building at varying scales (from peephole to building-size display case). Passing beyond the glazed gallery space and out into the courtyard the visitor moves below the section of the cabinet in which the educational facilities are housed. This slides out past the edge of the glazed gallery, blurring its boundary and engaging with the space beyond. The bookshop and café/restaurant have an immediate relationship with the public open spaces and can use them in a direct way.

foyers and connections

The principal foyer is positioned adjacent to the entrance from via Nizza. It is considered as continuous with the event-space, conference area, and other facilities behind. Swinging screens permit the space to be partitioned in multiple ways and allow the various properties of the programmatic elements to the be drawn into the general architectural field of the space below courtyard/garden level: the projection facilities of the conference room, for example, can become part of the event and exhibition space. Thus the foyer can have an immediate and unbroken connection with the exhibition and performance spaces that lie behind it. From the principal foyer immediate access is available to a 'secondary foyer' (and consequently to the library, bookshop café/restaurant, and education facilities around it) by means of the 'beam' which crosses above the event space. To move from the foyer to the long exhibition space in the building fronting onto via Cagliari, the visitor bears to the left, passing below the ramped ground plane that rises to courtyard/garden level. This space is announced by a glass casket held within the first bay, in and out of which the vertical circulation rises. Direct access is also available from the foyer to the exhibition space in the building held above it (facing via Nizza).

event and exhibition spaces

The event-space lying beyond the foyer is a complex architectural field which has permeable boundaries and which operates in a series of levels. It is an archive of the movement of the cabinet: the density of its traces are deposited and conserved here. The boundaries of the space can, however, be closed and a series of more conventional spaces established. The event-space is lit by the incisions in the ground plate above. The exhibition area in the building fronting via Cagliari is a tall, top and side-lit space. At high level, a walkwa runs along its length, giving access into the artists' ateliers which float above the exhibition area. Light enter through glazed slots between these. Visitors standing in the courtyard/garden and looking into this area have a long and deep view into the space. The exhibition area in the building looking on to via Nizza (which is accessed vertically from the foyer, or from the stairs or elevator and walkway in the via Cagliari building) has a more intimate character: here there is a greater sense of removal from the city and public spaces below. In its opening the cabinet also constructs a series of exhibition spaces of varying scales which are viewed from the public spaces of the courtyard/garden as they unfold through the site and pass through the existing glazed gallery.

metis   urban cartographies

bar/café and restaurant

Entering from via Cagliari, the visitor walks toward the bar/café and restaurant. To the visitor's left a long bar stretches out, contained in a one-storey linear building which is held up above the delivery access ramp. In front is the restaurant, on two levels. A folding glass screen allows the lower floor to open directly on to, and become part of, the courtyard/garden. The bar/café and restaurant have a direct visual relationship with the street.

bookshop

The bookshop faces the bar/café and restaurant, on the ground floor of the cabinet piece that contains the library (above) and the multimedia resource (below). Through the bookshop, access can be gained to the minor staircase (intended primarily for artists) that gives access to the walkway that runs along the via Cagliari exhibition space. The bookshop is directly adjacent to the 'secondary foyer' and hence to the route which connects the café/restaurant, bookshop, library, and educational facilities to the principal foyer by way of the 'beam' running over the event-space.

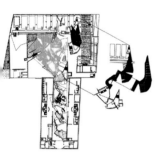

library and archives

The library occupies the two floors in the cabinet piece above the bookshop. Offices for staff occupy a mezzanine level on the upper of these two floors. They emerge through the upper surface of the cabinet, exploiting the available views and light. The archives are positioned in the sliding cabinet pieces behind the main library consultation room. Here there is a dense deposition of material within the cabinet. Access is controlled through a single door. The route of the archive spaces connects into the educational facility by way of a small office space/reading room. The reading room for rare materials is situated at the top floor of one of the archive cabinet pieces. The space is top lit, and each desk has a small window that is integral with the desk and which projects though the skin of the cabinet. The library area is positioned in close proximity to the bar/café and restaurant.

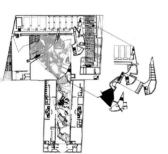

educational areas

The educational facility is linked, through a controlled office area, to the archives. It is double height, with a mezzanine. Light comes from above through light-catchers based upon the urban grain which this section of the cabinet represents. There is direct access to the educational facility from the courtyard/garden by the public staircase which also gives access to the exhibition spaces contained within the refurbished stables buildings.

metis   cabinet of the city

sectional development

event-space and foyer   gallery walkway   ground plate   cabinet elements   laboratory-ateliers

event-space and foyer   gallery walkway   ground plate   cabinet elements

via nizza

1. entrance via nizza
2. electronic information
3. ramp to courtyard
4. primary foyer
5. information centre
6. event-space
7. glass bridge / beam
8. contemporary art exhibitions
9. secondary foyer
10. information
11. multimedia
12. depots
13. loading bay
14. depots / storerooms
15. service ramp
16. laboratories
17. permanent collections
18. conference hall
19. cloakroom
20. ramp to car park
21. creche
22. guard's changing rooms
23. hospitality room
24. guest accommodation

plan (via nizza entrance:0.00m)

ia nizza ramp and foyer

entry-space with glass bridge / beam

metis   **cabinet of the city**

study collections/experimental areas/laboratory-ateliers for artists

These areas for artists are situated off the high-level walkway in the via Cagliari exhibition space. Conceived as wooden structures inserted within the existing structural bays, they project above the parapet edge, their smaller domestic scale and repetitive character intimating housing and inhabitation when seen from the street. They are double-height with a mezzanine level and are lit through retractable glass roofs with louvres. Below the mezzanine platforms are small kitchens and study areas.

conference hall

The conference hall is part of the architectural field of the event-space lying beyond the principal foyer. Using swinging screens it can be turned into an enclosed and autonomous space. When open, its projection and technical facilities can be used in events and exhibitions.

guards' changing room and guest accommodation

Both the rooms for the gallery guards and the accommodation for guests are directly accessible from the primary foyer. They are stacked above one another and are reached by the stair and lift lying between the cloakrooms and the conference area.

laboratories

The laboratories are situated beside the loading bay and the depots.

depots-storerooms and access patterns

Vehicular access for deliveries is by the ramp that leads from via Cagliari and which descends below the bar/café. This opens on to a general storeroom and depot area from which material can be transferred directly to the event-space area, to the via Cagliari exhibition spaces, and, by way of a service elevator, to the exhibition spaces contained in the former stables buildings. The restaurant kitchen is connected by stair and service elevator to the delivery zone.

guards' changing room and guest accommodation

Both the rooms for the gallery guards and the accommodation for guests are directly accessible from the primary foyer. They are stacked above one another and are reached by the stair and lift lying between the cloakrooms and the conference area.

parking

The ramp from via Nizza leads to the two levels of underground parking. The parking layout spirals around the site, outside the lower levels of the central event-space. It passes underneath the delivery point and depots.

visual arts research and documentation centre

The Visual Arts Research and Documentation Centre is located on the courtyard/garden level of the two former stables blocks, from where it has an immediate connection with the space of the glazed gallery. As the cabinet unfolds through this space, it leaves a trail of programmatic and exhibition elements leading to the education facility housed in the cabinet element that slides out from the glazed gallery space into the courtyard. The glazed gallery is lined with activities relating to the research and documentation projects carried out by the institution.

general administrative offices

These are located in the area in which the existing library is situated. They have a close functional connection with the activities centered around the glazed gallery.

exhibition galleries for the permanent collection

The two rooms on the first floor of the former stable buildings, together with the four on the second floor, are reserved for the permanent exhibition of modern art. The existing circulation within these spaces connects them to a new gallery level below the glazed courtyard. This new gallery level has a connection (by a ramp, derived from one of the cabinet pieces) to the principal foyer. The existing vertical circulation is supplemented by a new public entrance, staircase and elevator held within a cabinet piece immediately at the end of the glazed gallery. This new vertical circulation also connects with the education facility. The elevator is scaled to transfer art works and provides a direct passage between the depots and storerooms below and all gallery levels. The penetration of the cabinet pieces through the ground plane of the glazed gallery introduces a patterning of light derived from the choreography of the unfolding cabinet.

cabinet passage

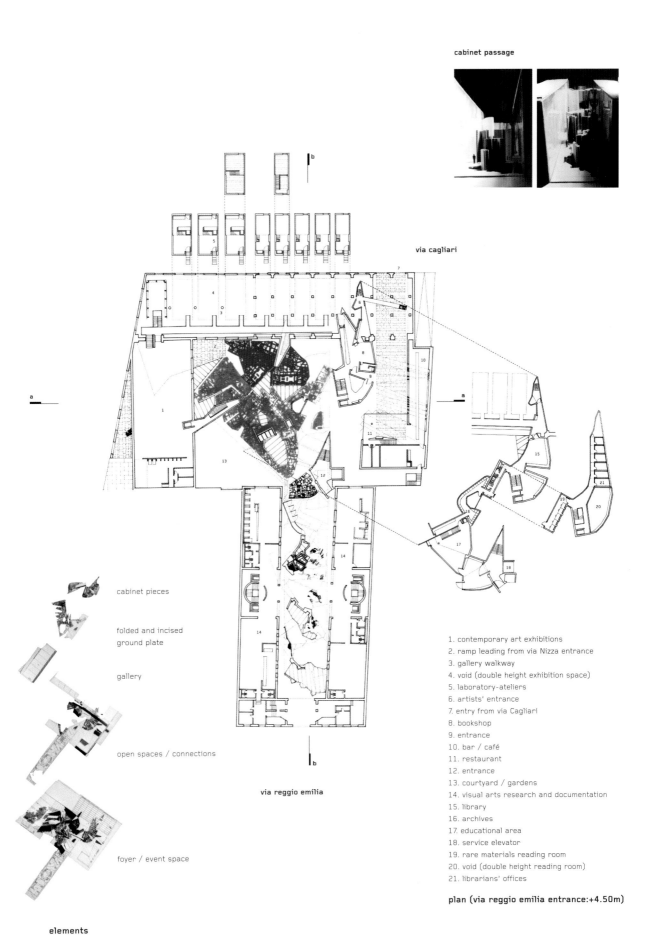

via cagliari

via reggio emilia

elements

cabinet pieces

folded and incised
ground plate

gallery

open spaces / connections

foyer / event space

1. contemporary art exhibitions
2. ramp leading from via Nizza entrance
3. gallery walkway
4. void (double height exhibition space)
5. laboratory-ateliers
6. artists' entrance
7. entry from via Cagliari
8. bookshop
9. entrance
10. bar / café
11. restaurant
12. entrance
13. courtyard / gardens
14. visual arts research and documentation
15. library
16. archives
17. educational area
18. service elevator
19. rare materials reading room
20. void (double height reading room)
21. librarians' offices

plan (via reggio emilia entrance:+4.50m)

metis   cabinet of the city

cross section aa

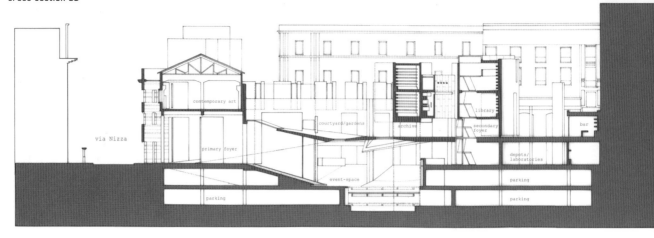

exploded axonometric of archive cabinet piece

the city within the cabinet

At all times the structure of the city that is embedded within the cabinet informed its operation and morphology. In a constant oscillation between scales, streets become seams, joints, or incisions, and buildings transform into stairs, tables and drawers. In the archive building below the rare document reading room, for example, the texture of a part of the city is used to define modes of storage. Metaphorically books, documents, manuscripts, photographs and paintings are sedimented within the grain of the city. Conceptions of city as text and text as city meet in a Borgesian conception, but one in which Rome itself is the labyrinth.

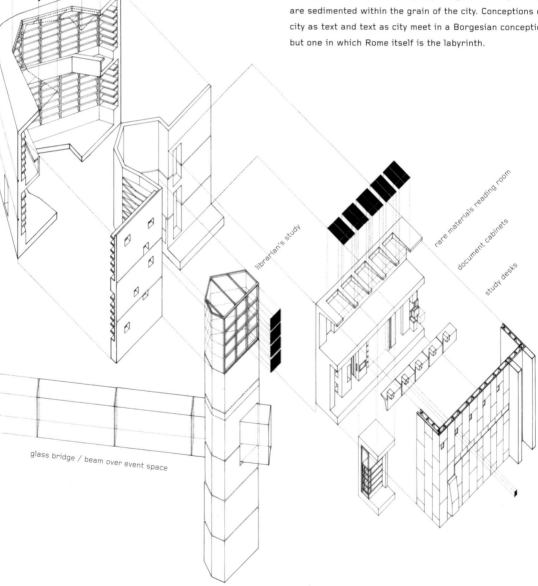

metis   urban cartographies

aerial view of cabinet in the urban block

cross section bb

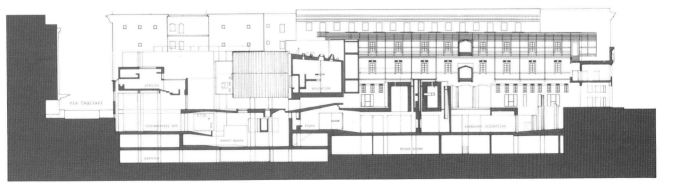

metis   cabinet of the city

the unfolding of the cabinet

91

metis

Mark Dorrian is a Senior Lecturer at the Department of Architecture at the University of Edinburgh where he runs the second year of the Master of Architecture programme and lectures in Theory and Historiography of Architecture. His writing has been published in *Artifice*, *The Journal of Architecture*, *Word & Image*, *The Journal of Narrative Theory* and *Chora*. He has received awards from the British Academy, the Graham Foundation, and the Canadian Center for Architecture, where he held a visiting scholarship. He is co-editor, with Gillian Rose, of *Landscapes and Politics* (forthcoming, Black Dog Publishing, 2003).

Adrian Hawker lectures at the Department of Architecture at the University of Edinburgh and teaches in the first year of the Master of Architecture programme. He studied at the AA and has taught in the USA, Australia and Germany. Working with Jenny Lowe, he was a finalist in the Federation Square art complex competition for Melbourne. He has won many awards and commendations in other competitions including the Shinkenchiku residential design competition; and, with Metis, the Britannia Basin housing competition. His work has been exhibited in Dublin, Berlin, London, Tokyo and Melbourne.

metis   biographies

Project Credits

britannia basin: Mike Shaw

mimetic urbanism: Andy Jones, Mike Shaw

cabinet of the city: Emma Carr, Sharon Giffen,
Akiko Kobayashi, David Mathias

Photographic Credits:

Patricia and Angus Macdonald (p. 14)

David Walker and PM Gallery & House (p. 17)

This book was published with the financial
assistance of the Department of Architecture,
University of Edinburgh

Acknowledgements

The work in this book has been produced while we have
been teaching at the Department of Architecture of the
University of Edinburgh. We are grateful to our friends
and colleagues there and to our students who have
often stimulated, and extended in their own work, the
ideas developed in these projects.

For much appreciated comments, conversation,
encouragement and help – of various kinds – thanks
to Atelier Big City, Andrew Benjamin, David Cottington,
Martina Frank, Susannah Hagan, Jonathan Hill,
Hugo Hinsley, Phyllis Lambert, Elizabeth Lebas,
Scott Lee, Daniel Libeskind, Graham Livesey,
Duncan McCorquodale, Indra McEwen,
Shane O'Toole, Alberto Pérez-Gómez, Frédéric
Pousin, Gillian Rose, Peter Salter, Vladimir Slapeta,
Kate Soper, Peter Tagiuri, Pieter Uyttenhove,
Marina Warner, Sarah Wilson and Jane Yeoman.

Thanks to Mike Shaw for lending us his superb
computer skills (and air miles); and to Stephen Cairns
for some important eleventh hour comments.

Metis' 'third (wo)man' is the artist Victoria Clare
Bernie with whom we have taught and talked for five
years. Over this time she has freely shared her
knowledge, insight, humour and superb organisational
skills with us and we owe her much.

Two people in particular stand at the beginning
of this work: Bill Carswell and Jenny Lowe; they
'brought us the plague'... but we realised it and
are grateful to them.

And, above all, thanks to Jane, Sebastian, JJ, Elizabeth
and Madeleine, to whom this book is dedicated.

Metis can be contacted at: The Department
of Architecture, University of Edinburgh,
20 Chambers Street, Edinburgh, Scotland EH1 1JZ.
Email: info@metis-architecture.com

© 2002 Black Dog Publishing Limited
and the authors

Designed by Gavin Ambrose
E gavin@dircon.co.uk

Printed in the European Union

Architecture Art Design Fashion History
Photography Theory and Things

Black Dog Publishing Limited

5 Ravenscroft Street

London

E2 7SH

UK

T 44 020 7613 1922

F 44 020 7613 1944

E info@bdp.demon.co.uk

British Library Cataloguing-in-Publication Data.

A catalogue record for this book is available from
the British Library.

ISBN: 1 901033 53 8

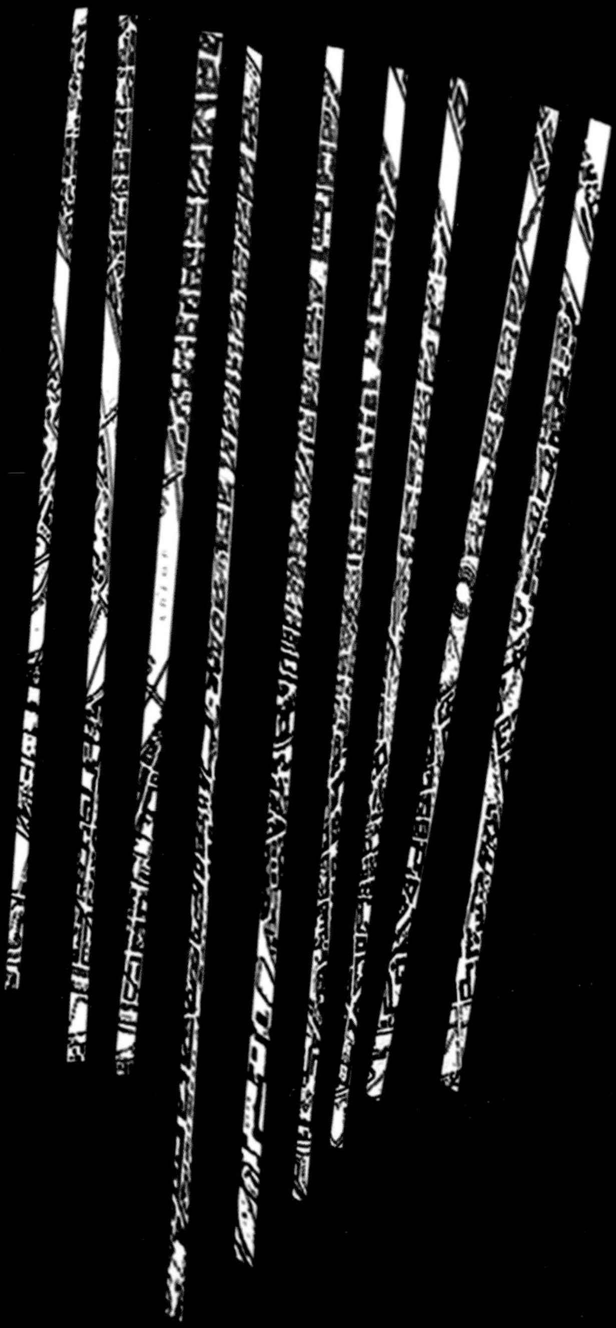